LOW MOOR

.....the beginning of a journey

Norman Ellis

Published by Low Moor Local History Group, Bradford
c/o 13, St Abbs Fold, Odsal, Bradford BD6 1EL - 01274 673274

1

Acknowledgements

I acknowledge with many thanks my indebtedness to Geoff and Mary Twentyman, whose help in preparing the typescript for printing was absolutely invaluable and to Joan Waddington who checked the final document before printing.

I am grateful too, to Eric Slicer for the advice and practical help in photographing some of the existing locations mentioned in the text

Finally, to the many friends who, by their interest and conversation have confirmed or amended some of my memories. Thank you!

First published April 1996

ISBN   0 9527427 0 5

Printed by Imprint, Keighley

CONT

AUTHOR'S NOTE

This is the second book that I have written. The first, 'TOWARDS LITTLE GERMANY', was based on my experiences after leaving school and starting to earn a living.

Whilst awaiting publication of that book, I felt the urge to occupy some of my time by writing a second book, this time about LOW MOOR and my experience of growing up in the village, between the years 1910 and 1926. I have called this second book 'LOW MOOR - THE BEGINNING OF A JOURNEY'.

This is not a book about faith and religion, but it would not be a true record if there were not, within its pages, some unmistakable signs of these Christian influences upon my life, and for which I now thank God!

This book is for my grand-daughter Harriet.

4

FOREWORD

by Rev Canon Donald Brown of Holy Trinity Church, Low Moor.

When I first met Norman Ellis nearly thirty years ago, Low Moor was beginning to change. Now the cottages and back-to-back houses of the Hill Top area have largely been demolished and replaced, the ironworks and the mill have gone, and green places where Norman played as a youngster have been built over.

Norman has dipped into his memory and recalled people and places and customs that have largely disappeared, and has had the initiative and expertise at 85 to put them on paper before they are forgotten. He has provided many a homely touch about a past community and way of life, and filled out a bit of local social history. I have been very interested to read his reminiscences, and wish I had his memory.

Donald F Brown

Thanks are due to Allied Colloids Group PLC who have generously sponsored the printing of this book.

Profits from this book will be donated to Help the Aged

ONE

GROWING UP ON FOUNTAIN STREET

I was born on the 10th of November 1910, at 36, Park Road, Low Moor, which was the home of my paternal grandparents, Garfitt and Sarah Ellis. They had previously lived at the bottom of Abb Scott Lane in what was then called Carter Fold. When and why they moved to Park Road, I have no idea, but after my parents were married, they lived with my father's parents for a while, certainly until I was due to appear on the scene. I think it is possible that up to that time my mother, who came from Storr Hill, was working as a weaver, but whether at one of the mills in Wyke or Low Moor, I do not know.

When I was born, my mother was attended by local midwife - 'Nurse' Coulson - as she was known by everyone. She was a well-respected woman and consequently she was in constant demand to attend confinements; but 'Nurse', except as a loose description of her profession, she most probably wasn't. That she had any certificates or diplomas is extremely doubtful, but she did possess a caring skill which, for the expectant mothers of Low Moor, counted far more than those tokens of a midwife's competence.

She lived at the end of Victoria Street in a house which projected beyond the line of the rest of the houses on that side of the street. Her grandson lived with her and he was known to us as Harold Coulson, though later it appeared that his real name was not Coulson but Ballinger. I may have been mistaken about this, but I think that such confusions did occur sometimes, when children were brought up by a relative other than by one of the parents.

We were a strong, chapel-going family so of course I was baptised according to the rites of the Primitive Methodists by William Warburton, a Local Preacher, and I believe, a Councillor at the time, later to become an Alderman.

My first real awareness of the house where I lived was the one in Fountain Street. My parents probably set up home there shortly after I was born. At about the same time, my grandparents, as a matter of good house keeping no doubt, since there was now just the two of them, moved to No 8, Tyrrel Street, a house owned by local butcher Harry Hood, whose shop was in Mill Street.

The house in Fountain Street was a back-to-back, and our windows faced on to the street. The houses at the back were reached by means of a 'landing', with railings as a necessary safety measure. This landing ran the length of the four houses.

Because the houses were built on quite a steep slope, a row of single-room cottages had been built underneath the houses which were behind ours, and the people who occupied those cottages were said to live 'under t'landing'.

My Aunt Carrie was one such occupant. She lived there with her mother who was an invalid, and I don't remember that she ever spoke to me from her sick bed. Apparently I didn't expect this to happen, either; perhaps she was so ill that she was incapable of speech. When Grandma eventually died, my Aunt continued to occupy the house for a year or two afterwards.

I have seen photographs of back-to-back houses in other parts of the city which were of similar design, though I don't suppose that they were very popular, with rows of toilets (or W.C.s) being located in all sorts of odd corners.

I recall, with some surprise, playing around the foundations of a house that was actually being built on the only available space left in Fountain Street, at the bottom of the slope, with the back of the new property and the house next to it, being separated from the backs of the houses in Victoria Street by a low wall, the resulting space being used as a dump for all kinds of rubbish. I can still remember the smell of the quicklime as the building progressed. The year, I think, was 1914. just before the commencement of the war.

Although I was probably no more than four years of age when we left Fountain Street for Moor Top, a move hastened, no doubt, by the birth of my sister; I can still remember the names of so many of our neighbours.

This word 'neighbours' really meant something in those days. Whatever difficulty a family might find itself in there was always a neighbour ready to help, with washing, ironing, baking, looking after the children, or perhaps simply raising a neighbour's washing-line, as it stretched across the street full of newly-washed clothes, to enable the 'pop-man' or the coal-man with their horses and carts, to pass along the street.

Sometimes 'Salt Jim' used to come along the street with his donkey and flat cart, hawking his blocks of salt, or more frequently, lumps chopped from the blocks. He couldn't be said to have been a very regular visitor and if my memory is to be relied upon, he only appeared two or three times a year.

It was quite a common sight, in those days to see street singers (beggars, really, I suppose) walking the streets singing well-known hymns; not the popular songs of the day, but popular hymns that they had probably learnt at various Salvation Army Hostels. Scarcely a week passed that one of these gentry didn't appear on our street. I remember that 'Lead, Kindly Light' and 'Abide With Me' seemed to be favourites with many of these 'down-and-outs'.

Most mothers, even in those hard times seemed not to be averse to sending their children out to drop a copper into the cap of the tramp/vocalist, although knowing full well that it would be surprising if it failed to reach the hands of the nearest publican- and quickly.

In the pre-school days, or during holidays from the Infant's School, there was always some interesting activity taking place on our street.

Hawkers used to appear quite regularly, and went along each street in turn, selling their goods from small suitcases, carts and vans, but the one I liked the best was the 'Yeast Man'. He came along the street carrying a basket on his arm, which contained his yeast done up in twists of newspaper, some two ounces and some four ounces. His name was Zena Bottomley, and everyone knew him, of course, as he walked the streets, ringing his little bell.

In those days every self-respecting housewife did her own baking. Whatever the size of the family, the housewife baked the bread for the week. For some it would be four loaves and a dozen teacakes, as well as a sponge cake, or occasionally a seed cake. For larger families (and families of six or seven were fairly common), perhaps a week's baking meant a dozen loaves.

Zena Bottomley lived in Union Road opposite the end of Victoria Street, in a red brick house, which was quite outstanding for the area, due to its colour.

The house is still standing, but it is now a stone or cream colour. There were lots of other interesting characters who came along our streets, all of whom helped in their own small way, to make life in Low Moor what it was, eighty years ago.

The drapery van used to come round about once a week, although I think it was after we had left Fountain Street that I remember that the salesman was Harry Metcalfe, my mother's cousin, and a well-known local baritone singer from Oakenshaw. He used to call at our house and eat his dinner with us while on his weekly round.

It was quite usual to see a chimney sweep with his bicycle and brushes, as well as his statutory soot-blackened face. Walter Sutcliffe was perhaps the one I remember best, who lived on Collier Gate, not far from another well-known character - Edgar Benn, who was blind, though not totally blind as he was able to make a sort of living by selling and delivering newspapers. There was another blind man whom I used to see quite often, usually going up or down North Street, with the assistance of a white stick. I don't think I ever knew his proper name, but he was always known as 'Blind Dick.', the adjective being pronounced to rhyme with 'Tinned'. He probably used to live somewhere on Manor Row.

Another itinerant vendor was the photographer who came around from door to door, offering to take family photographs, mainly of children, I suppose. The photos were taken, developed and printed all in the space of a few minutes. They weren't of today's standard, of course, but I have one or two such photographs somewhere about the house which are still recognisable pictures of me, taken nearly eighty years ago.

It seems ages since our street lamps were lit by gas, and almost unbelievable that they had to be lighted by a man walking around with a ladder on his shoulder and with a pocketful of matches. Such was the case, however, and I remember that the local lamplighter also operated as the local window cleaner. His name was Firth; there were a lot of Firths in Low Moor. I think HIS name was Arthur.

There were several Walter Firths, one of whom was the 'potman', who lived in Common Road almost opposite the Infants' School. He sold all kinds of household and kitchen wares, especially pots and pans, etc.

I was probably about three years of age when I started at the Low Moor Infants' School. We were living in Fountain Street when I was taken to school for the first time, but it wasn't long before I had to make the longer journey from Moor Top, and after a short while I was able to tackle this extra distance, unaccompanied by an adult, but along with my friend William Stobart, who was almost the same age as myself and who lived in Cemetery Road.

The highly respected head teacher at the Infants' School was Miss Briggs, the other teachers being Miss Sucksmith and Miss Speight. I don't remember much about my first couple of years schooling, but I do remember being brought out to the front one day, along with a girl - Alice Sugden - as being the two best singers in the class. I apparently didn't find this special treatment at all surprising as my dad was a singer himself, and he used to accompany my early efforts at singing songs, on the piano at home.

I don't know why it made any impression upon me, but I did like to sing the old patriotic song 'The Death of Nelson', with its well-known line - 'ENGLAND EXPECTS'..ETC. We were living in the days of fervent patriotism, so perhaps this song was one that we sang at school. I think the song had ceased to be popular years earlier, if it ever was, but I remember that we had a copy of the music at home, so it came out now and then.

TWO

TRAGEDY - THE LOW MOOR EXPLOSION

On the 21st of August 1916, I recall that we were brought face to face with tragic reality. I was playing with my cousin and a few other children in Hope Street.

I don't remember hearing the noise of an explosion, but suddenly the street was alive with mothers and grandmothers running back and forth, calling for their respective charges and hurriedly whisking them away. I haven't the slightest idea what happened to my playmates, but when my grandma grabbed my hand and cried 'Come on', I went.

I had no wish to argue with my grandma, few people did, as I realised when I was older. First of all though, she rushed me through the park with me clinging on to her hand (we were living at Moor Top by this time), to join my mother and my baby sister, who was now almost two years old.

There was pandemonium all around, everyone being told by someone to 'GET AWAY', 'GET AWAY.' Soon we were joined by my Aunt Carrie and her invalid mother who was very frail, I remember. After a kind of 'Council of War' was held, it was decided to make for the open space of the cemetery, first of all. So, wheeling my baby sister in a push- chair and helping my Grandma Metcalfe as much as possible we made our way into the cemetery where we all sat down on the main promenade, having no idea what to do next.

As we sat there looking down towards Morley Carr there was no doubt in our minds about the gravity of the situation, as explosion followed explosion and huge balls of flame shot into the air; it was clear that the Low Moor Chemical Works was the scene of the disaster.

I am sure that most of us were aware that that was the place where explosives were handled and where munitions were made. Everyone, even the children of the locality, knew the men who worked on munitions, for the simple reason that as they made their way back to their homes after working a shift at the chemical works they were easily recognisable as men who worked with Picric Acid which was used in the manufacture of explosives, because their faces were dyed a deep yellow colour, and we saw quite a number of these operatives, of course.

It was only later, much later that it was explained to me that the great balls of fire that we had seen quite clearly from our position in the cemetery, were caused by flying, red-hot pieces of metal and brick from the explosions at the Chemical Works piercing the gas holders and igniting the contents. Whilst we could see the result of the explosions, we had little idea of the death and destruction that was taking place. The adults among us could only hope and pray. All the time that we sat there the cry was still 'GET AWAY', 'GET AWAY', 'YOU MUST GET AWAY'. What was my mother to do with a baby and an invalid mother?

I have no idea how it came about, because so many cars, (even for those days) and other forms of transport were travelling quickly up Abb Scott Lane, but it now appears that someone was in charge, marshalling the few cars which had available seating. Our relief can be imagined when we were told that a car was waiting to take us away from the danger area. Leaving the baby's push-chair right there on the promenade, we were all somehow crammed into a small car and taken to relatives at Shelf, where we spent the night.

When my father arrived home from work, the local grocer, Henry Barraclough, whose shop was at the top of Shaw Street, had of course, stayed with his shop and he was able to tell my father in which direction we had gone, so he guessed straight away where our sanctuary was likely to be - his cousin's at Shelf.

He began by walking first of all through the cemetery and very soon saw the push-chair still standing there, so he said to himself, he told me later, 'That's mine, I'm taking it'. And he did.

He carried on to Shelf where he joined the rest of the family. Later on, my grandparents arrived from Tyrrel Street; and now we really were ONE BIG UNHAPPY FAMILY.

That night the children were able to sleep in beds but there was no sleep for the grown ups, none at all.

It was probably the following morning when we received permission to go back to our own homes. There was no damage, as far as I can remember, to any of the houses at Moor Top, but the news was that Morley Carr, Raw Nook and Wesley Place had suffered badly. It was later that we learnt the sad news that a large number of munitions workers had lost their lives, and there were also many injured.

I think that perhaps it was the following morning, or the morning after that, when my father took me with him down to Low Moor, because in the first place he needed to telephone his firm - the B.D.A.Ltd - and it was therefore necessary for him to go to the Low Moor Telephone Exchange which was in a house on Oxley Street, a couple of doors away from where my Uncle Herbert and Aunt Clara lived. It was just a small exchange, as can be imagined in those days, and the few lines were very busy, no doubt largely as a result of the tragedy which had had its effect on the whole city. Eventually, after waiting a while the number was obtained by the operator Gladys Wood, the daughter of Smith Wood the local plumber. She later became Mrs Dyson when she married.

I think it was a day or two later that my father took me down to stand on the ash hill which was removed nearly forty years later, to make way for one of Allied Colloids' earliest plant extensions at Low Moor.

There with my hand clasped firmly in my dad's, we looked down on a scene of devastation, with fire appliances and ambulances still making their way amongst the havoc of damaged buildings and leaking hose-pipes, which were still playing on the smoking ruins. I shall never forget some of those scenes of disaster. Surely the worst tragedy ever experienced by the people of Low Moor.

THREE

THE END OF THE LINE

Somehow life began to pick up again, though for the grown-ups it meant the distressing daily scrutiny of the Telegraph and the Argus, for news of war dead and wounded. Each newspaper had a page or sometimes two pages, of small photographs of the fallen and wounded, and, of course, the firemen and the munitions workers involved in the Low Moor explosion were featured as well.

I think it must have been about this time when, because adults were discussing family affairs and talking about departed relatives, that I began to be made aware of my background, and started to learn something about my relatives, especially about my grandparents.

My mother's younger sister, Aunt Annie, along with Uncle Willie and my two cousins Phyllis and Winnie, lived in Hope Street. Phyllis was a little older than me, while Winnie was nearer my sister's age. Uncle Willie worked at Rigby's Wire Mill before he went into the army. Aunt Carrie worked as a weaver at Victoria Mills, just beyond the end of our street. As my grandparents lived in Tyrrel Street, we all lived very close to each other.

My sister was only a baby when we were living in Fountain Street, and as a result I spent a lot of time at my grandparents' home. I loved them both dearly, but I was especially close to my granddad. I thought he was a lovely, kind man, and it is gratifying to me now to hear old people whom he taught in Sunday School many years ago, confirm quite voluntarily, that he really did have a very kindly disposition.

He used to be a blacksmith or farrier, and he worked at what was called by the locals 't'Wrights' Shop', part of the Low Moor Company, where horses were shod, wooden carts repaired and where wheels were made and fitted with their iron hoops.

These premises, which consisted of the blacksmith's shop, the stables and the timber yard, were at the junction of Abb Scott Lane and Huddersfield Road.

I think that at one time, when my father was living at home and my grandfather was working as a blacksmith, the family lived right next to the Low Moor Company's timber yard, in what was then known as Carter Fold.

I believe that at one time there was a dam at the back of Carter Fold, the water being used to supplement the supplies of the timber yard and the stables. I am not sure that I ever saw this dam, but in any case it was drained and filled-in a long time ago.

I have the faintest of recollections of visiting my grandparents when they lived in North Street; this is quite possible because according to the probate of my grandfather's Will, his address is given as 8, Tyrrel Street, formerly of 9, North Street. I assume that they moved to the North Street address after granddad ceased to work for the Low Moor Company, and before they occupied the house in Tyrrel Street.

These must have been very difficult days for them, and certainly very confusing for me, though I was much too young to appreciate the real nature of the problems of illness and unemployment.

This was the time that I vaguely remember them living in North Street. I was probably no more than two years of age. It was then that I recall seeing my grandfather setting off on his rounds from North Street.

He must, at that time, have been recuperating from his illness and able to go around from door-to-door selling fents and other small items which he carried around in a suitcase, in order to make enough money on which to live.

It seems that he had become ill with the dreaded disease Typhoid Fever, and as a consequence, lost his job when he was unable to work. How they, and other families in similar situations managed, I can't imagine; no Social Services, no Sickness Benefit. It must have been a real struggle for them.

Eventually my grandfather obtained a job as a road sweeper with the Corporation, which job he then held to the end of his working life. I used to see him sometimes when I was going to school, and when he was going about his labours, and I would ask him 'Have you got any 'taws' (marbles), granddad? He often had one or two in his pockets that he had found as he had swept along the gutters.

Sometimes, I remember that he was required to work on Tar Spraying, and this was, I believe, only on Sundays, presumably in order to avoid the

16

traffic(?). He used to let me try on the protective glasses with which they were issued and I remember that they smelt strongly of tar.

I remember well the days when we used to play in the 'Goit', which led from Royds Hall dam. There was a stream which ran down towards the bottom of Abb Scott Lane, and this stream probably flowed into the dam attached to the Timber Yard. Another stream in which we used to play, ran down the Common Road side of Potter Common, eventually to be lost somewhere at the other side of Huddersfield Road, where it helped to maintain one of the company's dams there.

One of the memories I treasure from the days when we were living at Moor Top, is that of seeing the appearance on a summer evening, of the Low Moor Company's horses, or perhaps they were Wilks's horses working for the Company, and being led, (and sometimes ridden by young lads), up Abb Scott Lane and Cemetery Road. We used to find it quite exciting to see all those heavy work-horses, perhaps as many as a dozen or more, galloping up the road to the fields where they were to spend the night after finishing their work for the day.

These were the fields that later became the Horsfall Playing Fields. Other horses were led up the long drive-way, past Royds Hall dam, to spend the night in the adjoining fields.

Earlier reference to Potter Common - the area which is now occupied by Delf Hill Middle School and grounds - reminds me of the fun we used to have climbing about on the huge rusting canopies, large wheels and other massive iron vessels and triangular frames which had been dumped there and which made for us a splendid activity centre, and the place where we enjoyed many hours of fun and excitement.

The wheel on its axle, which now stands on the corner of New Works Road and Huddersfield Road, is a reminder of the type of structure that used to be manufactured by the Low Moor Company. Why so many pieces of equipment ended their days on the Potter Common, slowly to rust away, I do not know. Of course this was in the days before such materials were collected for use in the manufacture of armaments during the years of the Second World War.

Potter Common was crossed by a footpath which ran from a point opposite the bottom of Park Road, across the common to a point near the bottom of Abb Scott Lane. It was a much-used short cut across to Huddersfield Road and to the Harold Club, but Potter Common was a place of interest to me for another reason too.

17

At the corner of Abb Scott Lane were the 'Coal Drops'. This structure had been erected so that engines could bring wagons full of coal from Low Moor Station, to be loaded into the wagons of the Low Moor Company and its agents, for distribution to the householders and other users in the area.

As young lads we found this whole operation most fascinating because there were so many aspects of the procedure that caused us to watch the different stages with the greatest interest.

To begin with, there was the old engine which used to pull the trucks from Low Moor Station, where the coal was loaded into wagons before beginning the short journey (which sometimes took a long time) to the Coal Drops at the bottom of Abb Scott Lane.

The reason why such a short journey sometimes took several hours to complete, was due to the fact that it was not unknown for the old engine, and sometimes some of the wagons too, to become derailed.

There was interesting activity for us to watch all along the line, wherever we happened to be, between Wesley Place and Abb Scott Lane, but the best place of all was to be down Cleckheaton Road when the disaster occurred. That was where, for some reason unknown to me, the derailment occurred most often. What an interesting struggle went on in order to get the engine, and sometimes a wagon or two, back on the lines.

The engine used to leave the Goods Yard, I believe, with, perhaps, three or four wagons full of coal, and coming up by way of Morley Carr, came across and on to the line which ran up Cleckheaton Road, by the side of the stream, which was just over the wall.

The old engine pulling its trucks full of coal, came puffing up the line, following Common Road and turning gently left past the local landmark, the Black and White Chimney. This, of course, was before the chimney was felled on the 12th of February 1921.

Huddersfield Road was then crossed by means of a level crossing, where one of the men would be required to dismount from the engine and, sometimes, wave a red flag in order to stop the traffic until the engine with its load had crossed the road.

If everything had proceeded happily thus far, the coal train would pass the 'Puncheon Lump' (the group of houses beside the track, which in reality boasted the title of 'MATHER'S BUILDINGS'), but no-one called them that except , perhaps, the postman.

Mrs Myers, in her book explains the unusual name by saying that in the days before bags had been brought into use, coal was carried in tubs or containers called 'Pancheons'. The emptied pancheons were dumped at the side of the track, the site becoming known as the 'Puncheon Lump'

Continuing past its real destination, the coal train would proceed to the end of the line, where the points would be changed to allow the engine to reverse and move the wagons slowly up the incline to the coal drops where the coal would be discharged into bunkers.

I remember these concrete bunkers being built and then being lettered by local artist Harold Bateman. This lettering stood the test of time for many years.

At the coal drops the Company's agents and customers would later collect their supplies of better or black bed coal, which was then weighed at the coal staith weigh office as they left the yard.

FOUR

EVERYBODY NEEDS GOOD NEIGHBOURS

I think it was shortly before we left Low Moor that my father became a member of the 'VOLUNTEERS', and wore, for drill and other parades, a uniform which was very similar to an enlisted soldier's uniform. He was never away from home for more than a few days at any time, but I remember quite clearly, the occasion when he was required to report for a weeks training, under canvas at Skipton. He was never called up for active service, I don't know why, perhaps he was just one of the lucky ones, for I don't think that he could have been considered to have been a Reserved Occupation.

I can just remember him discussing with my grandma the possibility of his being sent to the front, and his displaying the sort of bravado that young men do in such circumstances. If I remember correctly, his words were 'Well, if I have to go, Mother, I have to go.' I remember my grandma, from her sick-bed, (she was quite ill, with a heart complaint), chiding him in her Yorkshire accent 'Alfred. Ah'm varry low, you know.' She actually died in 1919.

There was a less serious occasion I recall, when my father, having been issued with a rifle as a member of the uniformed Volunteer Force, was demonstrating to us his knowledge of the drill that he had been taught.

With his rifle over his shoulder, he responded smartly to his own command 'About turn.', only for his rifle to make contact with a large ornament that stood on the mantlepiece which fell to the floor and shattered into many pieces of various sizes.

In those days of austerity, broken ornaments were not easily or cheaply replaced, so it was perhaps the first time that I witnessed 'Seccotine' being used for mending pottery. The vase remained on display for a long time, I recall, but no one was likely to suggest that it had been invisibly mended; its war wounds were too plainly visible for that.

Perhaps it would be appropriate at this point to recall, as well as I am able, the names of our neighbours in and around Fountain Street. I can still remember the names of a number of them, now long departed, whose grandchildren live away from Low Moor.

I think that the Beanland family, who used to live on the landing behind us, come first to mind. I believe they moved to Oakenshaw when they left Low Moor.

Living underneath them and next to Aunt Carrie was a Salvation Army lass called Lena. I used to see Lena from time to time, wearing her black straw bonnet with its red ribbons.

At the front and on the same side of the street as ourselves, was the Knowles family - Sarah, Lizzie and Willie. Willie Knowles' father used to work in the blacksmith's shop where my grandfather worked at one time, and I have a photograph showing Isaac and my grandfather in the same group in the workshop.

Also on Fountain Street and on the same side were the Booths, the Savilles and the Hills. On the opposite side of the street lived milkman Harker Shaw and his wife, with their daughter, Nellie. Many years later, Nellie married a mate of mine, Winston Breaks, who lived just a few streets away, at the end of Manor Row.

Further along Fountain Street, towards North Street, lived Mrs Wooler in a low cottage which was next to the short passage into Hope Street (and next to the W.C.s) and further along lived Mrs Read and her family. I don't remember a 'MR' Read, but I do remember Harry, Jack and Jennie.

Nearly opposite them were a couple of families who lived in houses with cellar-kitchens. One of those families was called Lee, I remember. Down the slope lived the Hellewells, who, it was rumoured, had been left a large sum of money, said to be £32,000, following which stroke of good fortune, they left the street and went to live on Halifax Road. I think that Walter Lightowler and his wife lived down the slope too, and there was also another family with two grown up sons who I knew very well, but whose names I seem to have forgotten, though I think one of the sons was called Sam. Right down at the bottom lived the Burgoyne family.

Although I have now forgotten the names of some of the families who lived in Hope Street, there are still a few names that come readily to mind, the first of which, obviously, is my Aunt Annie Harris, Uncle Willie and Phyllis. Winnie was probably born after we had moved to Moor Top. Freddie Sheddon, his wife and family lived on Hope Street, as did the Shoesmiths, the Ackroyds, the Kellets and the Wilmans.

I seem always to have known Gerry Wilman - whose given name is Harold - though he was always known as Gerry, and even his wife calls him Gerry today. I think he will be a good couple of years younger than me.

I knew his brother Percy, the eldest and Fletcher the youngest. In my early years, it was because of one of his hobbies, which made him popular with the local children. He used to fly hot air balloons at galas and similar functions.

These were tissue-paper balloons and I've almost forgotten the principle involved, but I think it concerned a pad being impregnated with methylated spirits and being suspended beneath the open end of the balloon. When this pad was ignited, the balloon filled with hot air, whereupon it rose towards the sky and floated away to the delight of the young spectators.

In North Street, and at the end of Hope Street and Tyrrel Street was the grocery stores belonging to the Thorpe's. I cannot remember that I was ever asked to go to this shop for any groceries - we were Co-op people.

Right at the very top of the hill, and at the corner of North Street and Manor Row, opposite the house where the Marshall family lived was the tiny sweet shop of Mrs Hirst. Now this shop I DID visit from time to time and purchased various sweets, such as 'Tiger Nuts' and 'Lemon Kali', with its short tube of licorice sticking out of the top of the yellow package. I believe that the Hirst's had a son named John, who was a pianist.

At the other end of Tyrrel Street, between Union Road and Park Road, was the Sargeant Dam. I think that this dam must have been an emergency supply for the mill. We used to enjoy playing round its banks, and sometimes, even trying to catch fish without much success. But, along with a number of my mates I used to get the most pleasure from this dam when it was frozen hard in winter.

That was the time when I used to pretend to skate, wearing my mother's old clogs; they were, however, very good on slides. This dam, like so many others has been drained and filled in, the land having been used for housing.

Even as a small child I noticed what a large number of butcher's shops there were in Low Moor. I recall that there was even a slaughter-house in School Street at one time. Butcher's shops, fish and chip shops, public houses a-plenty. I suppose that it could reasonably be argued that the hard-working men of Low Moor, (and who could deny that's what most of them were) needed a lot of food - and drink - to enable them to earn their daily bread.

Who would believe, though, that Low Moor once boasted a jeweller's shop, and during my life-time too? Very few, I suppose, unless they had actually seen the shop for themselves, years ago. I have a small box, in pristine condition, the kind of things that was supplied by jewellers when they sold a bracelet or a necklace, and the name of the jeweller is clearly printed on the box - 'SIMPSONS JEWELLERS'.

The shop in School Street, was the first shop on the right of the small shopping parade as you came UP School Street. It was next to a couple of houses which were themselves next to the entrance to the slaughterhouse, if I remember correctly.

Mrs Simpson came to live at Moor Top, just a few doors away from where we lived, probably when she retired from the shop. I believe her son was an accountant or something similar, because he taught me bookkeeping at Carlton Street Evening School, for a time, a few years later.

My grandparents lived in Tyrrel Street, which made the street very important for me, but quite a few other residents of the street must have made an impression upon me as well, at that time.

Next door to my grandparents lived Lawrence Bailey and his parents. Lawrence was a year or two older than me. I believe his father worked for the Corporation Cleansing Department, and perhaps it was he who was responsible for my grandfather obtaining a much-needed job as a road sweeper.

The neighbours on the other side of the Baileys were the Lightowlers, Doris and her parents. For a while shortly after I came out of the RAF I sang in a quartet party with Doris. She was married to Wilfred Thornton the greengrocer who had the shop in School Street.

Charlie Smith and his family were well known to me. He had the clogger's shop near the bottom of Mill Street, where he worked with Agnes Barraclough's father - Joe Henry Fox. Also on that side of the street was another family called Bailey and the Walker family. James Walker I knew very well for a couple of years, but I lost contact with him after he had moved to Wyke. I knew his sister too, she was an active worker for the Salvation Army.

Further along the street were the Dennison's with their two girls, and the chief memory I have of them is that they were - father and daughters anyway - a very dark, or black-haired family.

On the opposite side of the street lived a woman whose name was Mrs Davis and she lived opposite my grandparents. I think that she had either her daughter or her granddaughter living with her. I have no recollection of there being a MISTER Davis.

At the end of Fountain Street, facing the entrance to the mill yard, were two shops; one was the fruiterer's shop owned by William Cursley, the other was a milliner's shop occupied by Mrs Cooper. She was a friend of my grandma, and on her retirement, lived in one of the houses up Union Road facing on to the land on which the Wesleyan Reform Chapel was built to replace the old 'Tin Chapel'. I am not quite sure who followed Mrs Cooper at the milliner's shop but I believe it might have been someone called Horrell.

I vaguely remember being taken by my grandfather to have my haircut at a barber's shop which, I think, was in part of the building which was known as 'The Jubilee Hall' on the corner of School Street and Union Road. I was not very old at the time, perhaps six or seven, but my memory is of a room that was perhaps, just a temporary barber's shop. The man who cut my hair was a member of a well-known Low Moor family named Hustler, and I think he had a lame leg. I don't remember his Christian name, but I think my grandfather knew him very well.

Some time later, Herbert Seed, in School Street, became my regular hairdresser and I went to him for a number of years. I remember I was going to him when he first started to use electric shears. I was always impressed though by some relics of a less sophisticated era. In the middle of the floor were several sawdust-filled spittoons.

It is difficult in these days perhaps, to imagine a situation in which on the streets of Low Moor were TWO ladies' hat shops, or I suppose they would be known as milliners. I doubt if they would be able to make a living today. I am not aware that even hat hire shops are to be found in Low Moor.

Not only do I remember a ladies' hat shop at the end of Fountain Street, but I remember another one which was on the corner of Victoria Square, in Huddersfield Road; and a strange sort of building it seemed to be, too.

I was most familiar with the gentleman's outfitters, the door of which was at the end of Wood Street. To enter this tiny, box-like 'emporium', you had to negotiate a couple of steps down into the bowels of the shop, where you were surrounded on three sides by ranks of shelves and drawers, all with neatly written labels on their fronts. This was the domain of 'MR' Flather, George Flather, while 'MRS' Flather, whom I'm sure my mother always called 'Lizzie Birkby' when in conversation with her friends and neighbours, had her hats on display in the milliner's shop above. This shop was entered, as I recall, by means of the doorway in Victoria Square.

Another shop that was important to me was that of Gill's newsagents, at the corner of Victoria Square and Lower School Street. My grandfather used to take me down to the shop at one period, probably a few weeks before Christmas, so that we could make weekly payments of a few coppers, for some toy or other that was 'put by'. For a number of years Ralph Gill's shop was an attraction for me because he sold so many children's books and toys, though on refection I believe that Brundill's in Huddersfield Road was equally popular.

Ralph's principal occupation though, was that of a printer, like his father before him. His printing machine was in the basement and there he did all kinds of printing for businesses and other organisations in the district, such as churches, chapels and Sunday Schools.

Hymn sheets were a speciality, as were decorated concert programmes. During the first world war, Ralph's father, Josiah Gill, would no doubt be kept busy producing such items, some of them being kept as souvenirs up to the present day.

It was 1935 when Ralph Gill left his shop and moved into his new printing works in Huddersfield Road, next to the Low Moor Working Men's Club which had only recently been built there. The new occupants of the newsagent's shop were Mr and Mrs Frank Thorpe.

FIVE

THE MILL AND THE SHOP

The Victoria Mills were a very important part of the life of Low Moor. Many of the young women of the district worked for one or other of the many different firms who were engaged in some stage in the production of cloth. The majority of them were spinners or weavers, and some, a much smaller number, I believe, were burlers and menders.

Most of the men who were employed at the mills would be overlookers, though some were engineers or 'Engine Tenters' as my grandfather would have called them. A number of older lads, especially those who were 'half-timers', worked in the weaving sheds as 'doffers'.

There was a system in operation, when I was young, whereby a boy of twelve, I think, was permitted to spend half a day at school and the rest of the day at a job such as that of a 'doffer' in a local mill. The work of the doffer entailed going round the looms when the weavers called 'Doff' or 'Doffer', collecting in a kind of basket on wheels all the empty bobbins and replacing them with full bobbins of 'weft'.

No doubt this system was looked upon with some approval by large families who found money hard to come by. I can't really say what effect the system had on the boys who were caught up in it, except that they never had the chance to take a scholarship examination to enable them to be considered for Secondary Education.

The Mill was always an interesting place to young lads, though there was little that we could see as we walked past. The dam at the other side of the fence in North Street was obscured by a high wooden screen which was covered, as I recall, in very faded red paint.

Because we were only able to get a glimpse of things through the mill gate, that were we to do in these circumstances, except walk through the mill yard? I don't remember that we were ever challenged, nor can I remember that we ever got up to any mischief in the mill yard, but it was a far more interesting way, even if it was not quite as direct a route from Fountain Street to the bottom of School Street.

Just inside the mill gate, and on the right, stood a W.C. like a lone sentinel guarding the entrance! I don't recall seeing any others, but surely there must have been some. Inside, sheltered from the wind and rain perhaps!

Straight ahead was one of the two dams, and this particular dam had what appeared to be a rather old-looking boiler which had been covered in pitch, to protect it from the elements, I suppose.It was mounted on some brickwork supports and from the front end of this boiler, and from a sort of swan's nest spout, issued a constant stream of warm water.

Turning past this small dam was the slightly larger one on the North Street side of the yard. One of the attractions for us, combined with the fact that the water always looked quite green in colour, was that, if we were lucky we might see one or two goldfish.

It probably wasn't long after I had become accustomed to walking up and down Common Road unaccompanied by an adult, that I began to be of some assistance to my mother running errands.

We had the one grocer's shop at the top of the street which we used frequently (especially when we asked for things to be 'put down', to be paid for later!). The shop was very convenient, of course, but Henry Barraclough didn't stock the range of products that were to be found in the shops in Low Moor, so my mother used to send me down to the Co-op for small items, if she had the money at the time, and I can still remember our Co-op check number - 1746! This number was recorded and in due course we would receive a bonus on the amount we had spent during the year. Everyone looked forward to receiving the annual bonus. Sometimes it made all the difference as to whether a new pair of shoes or a dress could be bought for the children.

To be asked to go to the Co-op was just a normal shopping exercise, but to be sent to Seth Briggs' shop - now that was an experience.

Seth Briggs was a Painter and Decorator and his shop, (if you could call it a shop), was at the bottom of Common Road, opposite his own house and the Police Station. It was a single storey building, originally two buildings, with the fewest and the smallest windows imaginable, consistent with its being the location of some human activity.

It was the darkest, the dingiest shop I ever went in to. Inside the doorway was a tiny counter, just to give the impression, as you stepped within, that you were entering a REAL shop. On the left was a store-room in which were dispersed various drums, barrels and carboys, together with all the other implements of the painter's profession such as ladders, brushes. ropes, buckets and dozens of opened and unopened tins of paint. Soft soap for washing stone floors, and cellar steps was another item that was obtainable from the shop.

For its size the tiny shop kept an amazing stock of products, ranging from children's remedies to cleansing fluids. Just occasionally I would be sent down to Seth Briggs's with a cup or a small jar, for an ounce (or was it two?) of Syrup of Violets.

We thought a great deal of this medicine at our house. Mother, because it helped to pacify my baby sister when she was teething, and me, because when I sampled it on the way back home (and I invariably did) I found its very sweet taste very much to my liking.

Mrs Briggs was usually in charge of the shop whenever I went, and I wondered how she found her way about - but she did. I suppose her eyes had grown accustomed to the gloom, but mine never did.

The shop had its own particular and peculiar smell, too. It met you as you put your nose inside the doorway - a mixture of the smells of oil, paint, tar, lime, disinfectant. and even perfume - I loved it.

SIX

A DETOUR AND A DUCKING

For years I had had to endure the sarcastic comments of some of my elder relatives and friends, concerning my lack of inches; a common expression that was used, supposedly to make me smile, was 'We s'all 'ev to put some hoss muck i' thi booits'.

Now that I was getting slightly bigger, (and braver), in order to get from Moor Top down to Low Moor, I had to get accustomed to walking down the 'snicket' - the long, and sometimes rather daunting footpath, which ran down to Common Road. The park wall on one side, and the boundary wall of West House, on the other for most of its length, sometimes made it a very gloomy pathway indeed.

West House was occupied by the wealthy mill owner and local benefactor, Alfred Briggs. At the top end of the snicket were the rear garden walls of about four of the properties in Abb Scott Lane; John Bryden's house being the uppermost, with the monumental mason's workshop (unused as such for many years), being next above, on the corner of Cemetery Road.

The workshop had at one time been used by Mrs Bryden's father, and the father of Harry Rostron, who also became a monumental mason; his house and workshop used to be at Rock House at the very top of Cemetery Road. Further down the terrace in Common Road lived Councillor J.W.Lightowler, well-known for his connection with Hill Top Sunday School, as well as for his Council work.

In the days before the National Health Service came to have such an influence upon our lives, health care was very much a DIY job. I remember rather vaguely our Doctors whose surgery was at Low Moor House. There was the much-loved Dr Robinson, and later his son, Dr 'Harry', who was always so sympathetic. Until her retirement, Miss Binns for many years dispensed, along with the doctors' prescriptions, kindness and cheerfulness of a very high order, and as a consequence she was greatly loved.

Payment for the medicines and for the doctors' services was, for so many families, (and we were no exception) on a deferred payments system. As a result, the doctors employed a collector to visit the patients' homes at regular intervals, perhaps weekly or fortnightly, to collect payments until the bill was paid.

Prescriptions were generally made up in the surgery by Miss Binns I believe. Such prescriptions when made up, were left at the home of Mrs Pickles in Lower School Street, from whom they were to be collected. I was aware that this was certainly the case with medicines for our family, and probably for all the families in that part of Low Moor too

It must have been a few years after we had moved to Moor Top that an incident occurred which could have brought my promising young life to a sudden end.

It was winter-time I remember, for the Park lake was covered with ice, and it was approaching dusk when my mother asked me to 'run an errand' for her by going across to Mrs Pickles's to collect a bottle of medicine, for whom, I don't remember.

This little task, which involved walking through the park carrying a shopping bag, and I wasn't expected to be more than half-an-hour or so. However, as I made my way along the promenade I could hear lots of noise and laughter coming from the direction of the lake, which was just through the trees on my right.

I couldn't resist taking the short cut down a little pathway, where I could see a number of young people, mostly a little older than me, enjoying themselves on a slide that was near to the edge of the lake. There were too many of them for me to want to join them, and I knew that I shouldn't waste too much time so I kept going, walking past this scene of youthful activity.

As I walked along the bank, I hadn't gone many yards before I came to a deserted slide. 'Wonderful.'I said to myself 'Just right for me'. It only took a second for me to step down on to the ice.

The slide looked shiny and most inviting; just a short run and I launched myself along the shining surface. Suddenly I shot through the ice up to my waist.

How was I to know that someone had thrown a piece of rock on to the end of the slide and made quite a large hole, which I just had not seen. Small wonder that no-one was using that particular slide. Luckily, because it was so near to the bank, I was able to scramble out, a very wet, very frightened boy.

Naturally, I abandoned the trip to collect the medicine, and instead, thought it would be quicker and wiser if I went to my grandparents' home in Tyrrel Street. I knew that I could face THEM, but I wasn't sure what my dad would have to say when he got home.

I believe I was put to bed after being thoroughly dried down. My grandfather collected the medicine from Mrs Pickles's, and then went to tell my parents what had happened. I suppose I would go to school the next morning from my grandparents' home, so that by the time I got home things would have quietened down bit, though I've no doubt that I was suitably reprimanded; but I have long since forgotten all about that.

I remember an occasion when William Stobart and I were returning home from a visit to Low Moor through Harold Park. We weren't very old, but our parents must have been able to trust us in the vicinity of the lake, no doubt because they expected that we would simply walk straight through on the promenade. Their confidence was, on this occasion, sadly misplaced and I was the culprit.

Near to the landing stage and the boats, the promenade used to slope down, and as far as I can remember, ended with a couple of yards of a kind of wooden platform up to the water's edge through which the water could be seen between the boards.

The lake at this point was not more than, say, ten or twelve inches deep, so there was no apparent danger and there wouldn't have been if, as we both bent over the water, looking for tiny fish, I hadn't given William a gentle push, just to see what would happen.

Of course, he fell into the lake. He wasn't too pleased, I recall, but he wasn't really very wet. He did wonder how it had happened, and, when he arrived home, so did his mother, no doubt.

Wherever there was water in and around Low Moor, we lads would always be attracted to it at some time or other. Summer, especially during the school holidays was the best time of all, when we would be able to visit every lake, pond and stream within a couple of miles of Moor Top. We knew where to find all the springs and wells in the area, and there seemed to be quite a lot of them, seventy years ago.

31

Speaking of wells reminds me of one particular well around which I and my young friends used to spend a lot of time and it was quite near home too, when we lived in Fountain Street. On the hill side, just above Manor Row, was the 'Dolly Well'.

Until very recently (May 1995) there were very few occasions when water was not bubbling out of the spring. Hundreds of children must have played around the 'Dolly Well' building walls, knocking them down, making channels to cause the water to flow in different directions. Sadly, there is nothing left now; all signs of this much-loved reminder of former days have been swept away by council workers within the last couple of months.

Another well which has almost disappeared is the one in the overgrown area just off Huddersfield Road near to Salisbury Road. I suppose it follows, now that the horses have gone, that the need for the wells no longer exists. I suppose this is true, but it's a shame, nevertheless.

Fishing was a great pastime. When we lived at Moor Top it was a matter of yards only to make our way to a choice of haunts. Our first choice, when we were very young, was the Fountain Pond, now no longer there, but it was just a few yards inside the main gates of Harold Park in Cemetery Road. It was filled-in and grassed or planted over, a long time ago. It used to have a fountain in the middle, but I am sure that I never saw this fountain playing.

All around the edge of the circular pond were large stones or small rocks that one could clamber amongst and sit on if you felt like it. A piece of stick or a branch from a tree, a length of cotton, a couple of match-sticks for a float, a bent pin, and you were a proper fisherman.

One other essential requirement of course, was a worm or preferably a tin full of worms. These were very easy to come by and the best and the juiciest, reddest varieties were to be found in a small tip where the park gardeners used to empty barrowfuls of weeds and other rubbish, just a few yards from the dam.

A float on your line wasn't really necessary, but it showed that you were an expert. As a matter of fact, most of the tiddlers, especially the 'bloodsuckers' that we caught, could usually be seen in the water, and all we had to do was to dangle the worm right in front of the fish's nose and raise the rod - one more tiddler for the jar.

Fishing in the 'Jug Dam',(a much larger pond up at the top end of the park), required more skill. Sometimes much larger fish being taken such as roach, perch, gudgeon and even one or two jack pike were to be seen occasionally; I remember seeing a pike taken on a spinner by Dan Laycock, a Moor Top lad who was a few years older than me, and a keen fisherman at that time. Mostly the lads and the older men who had decent tackle used to fish for roach.

The two principal places for real 'grown-up' fishing in our part of Low Moor, were Harold Park lake and Royds Hall dam. We youngsters used to try to catch the 'tommies', or roaches, which we could sometimes see lying between the stones on the bottom, near the edge of the lake. Mostly it was roach that the men fished for, but the odd pike was taken.

Pike fishing was much more common in the Royds Hall dam and far more likely to meet with some success than in either of the dams in the park. Some fishermen used to fish for roach in the park dam, and then go across to the Royds Hall dam, using the roach they had just caught, as live bait for pike fishing.

I remember the days when we used to go fishing, without rod and line but BY HAND. On summer evenings, when the air was warm and still, two or three of us used to gather by the corner of the park lake, nearest to Shaw Street and Cemetery Road. At these times it was usual for a quantity of debris to have collected in that small area, lying there on the surface of the still water, like a carpet.

Invariably there was action taking place below the surface, and this was indicated by the occasional disturbance of the debris; although we couldn't see them, we knew that some fish were playing there.

We used to lie on the bank and quietly wait for the moment when the water would be disturbed (No comparison with the sick at the Pool of Bethesda, intended - [see John ch 5].)

When we perceived the wriggling movement we used to plunge our hands into the water, to pull out a handful of leaves, and (because we had become rather clever at it) sometimes two or three small roach. The trick was to make, in one motion, a kind of scooping action which ended with a handful of leaves being flung on to the bank. Any small fish that were trapped amongst the leaves would be placed in a jar or a tin of water and kept for use by one of the pike fishermen as live bait.

33

SEVEN

THE TIPPLER

As a small boy, I remember being taken by my grandma to visit my dad's cousin, Hannah Maria Murgatroyd, who lived with her husband, Seth and son Harold, on Reevy Road, Wibsey; I suspect that grandma rarely went to visit my 'Aunt' Hannah Maria without taking me with her for company, and I was always very happy to go along with her. There were two reasons for this obvious eagerness.

Firstly, in order to keep me occupied, I was always provided (at my request) with an optical instrument through which I was able to view photographs which were specially prepared for three-dimensional viewing. I wasn't aware that the term was in use in those days, but I think the instrument was called a 'stereoscope'.

One looked at postcard-size photographs through two different lenses, with a kind of shade over the eyes, to keep out the light. The result was a realistic and life-like picture of different scenes which was guaranteed to keep me occupied for an hour or so, during which time the two ladies chatted away without interruption.

The second reason for my co-operation was the outside W.C. You may be saying to yourself 'What could be so special about an outside W.C., even seventy-five years ago?' Well, I will try to describe, as delicately as I can, the system which was, to me, a most unusual system indeed.

I believe it was known as a 'Tumbler' or 'Tippler' System and I've no doubt that it was considered to be quite a modern invention at the end of the nineteenth century, but I believe, hopefully, that the last of them was seen before the 1939-45 war. This system probably followed the old ash-pit or midden, and it must have been a considerable improvement on THAT.

The 'Tumbler System' worked (I think), on the principle that any water used at the kitchen sink for washing-up or whatever, would be carried by means of a pipe, from the sink to a kind of large bucket which was suspended over the space beneath an earthenware circular pan of about fifteen or sixteen inches in diameter, the pan being topped by a wooden seat.

When the quantity of water discharged from the kitchen had filled the bucket to a pre-determined level, the bucket tipped over, discharging its contents into the main drainage system.

This useful piece of equipment was housed in its own little abode in the small yard at the back, (hence the expression 'A'hm bahn aht to t'back'. My memory, perhaps a little flawed now after all these years, is of a small building or toilet, which had a smell which didn't always disappear completely, but it was certainly an improvement on the old dry closets.

Mention of those insanitary ash-pits reminds me of the hordes of flies that we used to encounter in days gone by, and which were associated, not least in my mind, with the conditions provided by the ash-pits.

At this time, which was around 1917-18 I suppose, most houses in the district had been supplied with the now familiar cistern flushing system, but I'm sure there were just a few of the old dry midden type closets attached to very old properties.

I can only remember one such hazard to public health, and one which I used only in the case of direst need. This was the men's closet, at School Street Methodist Sunday School, which was attached (of necessity) to the ash-pit at the bottom of John Street. This was in use (or disuse, depending on your sensitivities,) until the premises were vacated and the congregation moved down the street to Oxley Place Sunday School, following the collapse of part of the roof, in 1947. The Sunday School then became Oxley Place Methodist *Church*.

I am quite sure that there were far more flies about when I was a child than is the case nowadays; no doubt the end of the ash-pit has had much to do with the improved situation.

Although the danger to health posed by the house fly was recognised, efforts to eradicate it were, to say the least, rather half-hearted. Science, it seemed, had not really had the time to get to grips with the local problem of the house-fly, and when I was a boy quite ancient methods were still employed in some homes.

At first I used to wonder what this glass thing was, especially when it had just been cleaned out and replaced in the centre of the dining-room table. After a few hours in use, of course, it became quite obvious what the purpose of the object was - it was a FLY TRAP, as indicated by the corpses of the victims.

The fly-trap, as I faintly recall, was a bell-shaped glass jar, into which a cupful or so of beer or sweetened cold tea was poured. The flies were attracted by the sweet liquid, but after drinking their fill they were unable to find their way out again and were soon drowned in the attractive liquid.

We never possessed one of these objects at home, but I remember seeing one or two, usually in the homes of very old people.

Another method of catching flies, and one that was very popular when I was young, was by means of FLY-PAPERS. Almost every home and shop had them hanging from suitable locations such as gas brackets or pinned to the ceiling. They could be purchased at any general stores and a few may still be found today. They were in use from the arrival of the warmer days of late Spring to the onset of the colder days of Winter.

The fly-paper, when newly purchased, was rather like a photographic film, but approximately twice the width. When the paper was pulled out of its container though, unlike the film, its menacing capability was revealed, when it was seen that the film was coated on both sides with the stickiest form of glue imaginable. As a consequence, it needed careful handling by the householder or shopkeeper.

When in position, and with the paper pulled out from its container, any fly that was unwise enough to land on the sticky surface was unable to get free and so died there quite quickly. Sometimes, in shops especially, one would see a fly-paper almost black with the corpses of dead flies, so that, at times, there was scarcely room for another fly to land on the sticky surface.

Another memory that I have concerns my granddad again. It is only the vaguest of memories because I must have been very young indeed when I was taken by him to the upstairs room of what now appears to me to have been the Low Moor Liberal Club. I just remember that the back entrance and the living quarters were in Dale Street, and the front door was in Huddersfield Road. I can only imagine that at the time, perhaps in the period when he had no job following the typhoid fever attack, my grandfather took on this job, purely as a temporary measure.

I don't remember that the job was ever the subject of conversation in my hearing, but I was very young at the time. It appears that my grandfather was the curator or caretaker of the club.

I just recall that there was upstairs, what I later came to realize was a billiards table, and I cannot remember anything more about the club except that I remember that the room always had that strong and distinctive smell of tobacco smoke.

The club closed down some time later and the house became the residence of well-known Funeral Director - George Booth.

Talking about clubs - there were one or two others in this part of Low Moor. The Harold Club, of which my Uncle Herbert was a staunch member, was perhaps, the best known, but whether the bowling greens or the beer was the main attraction in his case, I do not know. Perhaps it depended on the season of the year, as he was quite a good bowler, with a number of awards to prove it. He was team captain I believe, at one time.

Next in popularity, to my Uncle Herbert, anyway, was the Low Moor Working Men's Club in School Street, which in my childhood was known as "t' Top o't'Street Club". It was well-known, of course, to everyone who worshipped at the PRIMS, being almost directly opposite the Chapel.

I suppose the relationship between the two organisations was as amiable as could reasonably be expected. I only remember entering the club on one occasion, and that was to take a message from my Aunt Carrie to my Uncle Herbert, her brother, and I remember climbing up some rather steep stone steps.

In August 1934 when the building had ceased to be used as a club, the members left the premises in School Street for their new building in Huddersfield Road.

The old club premises were occupied for a time by Wiley Bros., the screen printers, but when the nearby chapel became unsafe for public worship, it was offered for sale and bought by Wiley's.

The chapel congregation moved down School Street, joining up with the members of Oxley Place Sunday School, to form Oxley Place Methodist Church and Sunday School.

Another club which used to exist in Low Moor was the private gentlemen's club at the bottom of Thomas Street. It used to be called the Albert Club, but changed its name to the Ernest Club during the most recent days of its existence. I don't remember seeing much activity there, and I only knew the names of one or two of the members.

I referred earlier to the number of wells and springs that were to be found in the district; the sources of running water that I was most familiar with were those at various points between Carr Lane and Royds Hall Lane.

When I was young, these were all in regular use, some used by cattle in the fields and others by the roadside where they provided welcome refreshment for tired horses as they paused in the task of drawing heavy loads of coal and timber.

The one that I knew best, of course, was the Dolly Well, just off Manor Row, as I've already mentioned. No doubt this was once a spring which was used by animals in the fields, or by the horses pulling coal carts back and forth in the area of Hill Stones, but that was obviously a long time ago.

When my friend, William Stobart and I were attending Wyke Council School at about seven or eight years of age, if the weather was suitable, we used to walk to and from school, and I remember distinctly that on summer days, when we were on our way home, it was quite normal for us to jump over the wall and make our way to a well which was only a few yards from the road, and quite near to the tunnel which went under Huddersfield Road. The object of this slight detour was to enable us to plunge our heads in the clear, cooling water of the well, which activity refreshed us immensely and was most enjoyable.

The well just referred to was at the side of an old track which was an off-shoot from the track from Royds Hall down to St Mark's Church. This side-track entered the field next to Park Nook (now Low Royd) opposite the old vicarage. After passing under Huddersfield Road by means of the tunnel, the track continued across the fields where there was another well, and this I have cause to remember well(?).

William and I had, on one occasion been playing by this well and foolishly had been throwing stones into the well thinking that it was good fun to make the water splash out. Unfortunately, or perhaps fortunately, the farmer came along and caught us in the act. He took us along to the farmhouse, where his father - who I think I had heard my grandfather refer to as Paul Normington - gave us a 'good telling-off'. We certainly should have known better, and I'm sure we never tried that 'lark' again.

The construction of Woodside Road meant that the old pathway, the well and the tunnel were lost to sight for ever, to exist only in the minds of a decreasing number of old residents.

After leaving Hill Top Infants' School, William and I started at Wyke Council School, which seemed to be a very long walk for youngsters such as us, but it soon became a matter of little concern to us as we grew accustomed to the exercise.

If the weather was inclement, there was always the tram, but when we walked back home from school there was always a choice of interesting things to do on the way. For instance, there were the tops of walls to walk along, trees to climb, small caves in the hill side to investigate, and I remember that during the appropriate season, there were conkers to look for and acorns to collect from an oak tree which grew close to the garden wall of 'Park Nook'.

EIGHT

TABBED RUGS AND WOOL STOCKINGS

One of the memories that I have retained of the days when I was a scholar at Wyke School, was that, weather permitting, we were usually assembled in the playground in double lines, beginning with the smallest boys and ending with the tallest. I didn't like this method of drawing attention to my size, because I was always, for the first couple of years or so, the smallest boy in the class.

My partner, who was about the same size, was a fair-haired boy called Harker. We occupied those positions in assemblies and drill for a long time. I recall that the tallest boys seemed massive to me, like grown men. Once we got into our classrooms, however, such inequalities were of no importance to me.

I don't think that I was a particularly bright scholar, in spite of the fact that I did go on from Council School to Secondary School. This, no doubt was considered by my parents to be something of an achievement, at least.

I do remember that I was fairly good at one or two things; handwriting was one of them, and composition, as they used to call it, was another subject in which I was reasonably competent, and singing was yet another.

Perhaps it was about 1919 although I am not at all sure, but there was some kind of special examination and exhibition, with set exercises and displays in which I think the whole school was involved.

I recall that we were required to write a composition on a particular subject which I think was connected with the murder of the two young princes. I remember too, that I was taken on one side by the teacher and asked, as a special contribution, to write out in my very best handwriting, a few paragraph from my composition.

I probably thought no more about this task until some time later when my father was reading out from the 'Telegraph' about the activities that had been taking place in school, giving examples of the scholars' work. He read such a piece which I recognised at once as being my own work, and I remember saying quite emphatically 'I wrote that, Dad.' No doubt as a consequence of the incident I began to get the feeling that I was able to do one or two things rather well, which gave my self respect a much-needed boost.

This was revealed later, when the boys in my class were asked to contribute a few items for a class concert, possibly before breaking-up for the Christmas holidays. Instantly, without any sense of fear, I offered to sing a song.

I should mention at this point that my father, as well as being a member of the Wyke Glee Union, and the Choirmaster at our Chapel, was also a tenor vocalist, who did quite a bit of singing at various concerts, locally. I learned that he trained under Fred Healey of Wyke, who was probably the conductor of the Glee Union at that time.

Because my dad accompanied himself on the piano, when he was practising at home, I became very familiar with all his songs, and I came to know most of them - both words and music - almost as well as he did himself.

I didn't feel that there was anything at all odd about a nine-year-old boy singing a love song with the title 'LIKE STARS ABOVE', and which began with the lines:

> 'I SEE THINE EYES BEFORE ME
> LIKE BEACON STARS ABOVE.. etc.'

When the concert actually took place, (with no previous rehearsal), I recall that I had only just started to sing when the teacher stopped me, to say that I had pitched the song rather too high, and he then gave me a lower note on which to start again, which I did, quite unabashed.

I've almost forgotten what the reaction was, but I think that my effort was received with something approaching applause, especially from the teacher.

Later, the whole school assembled in the main hall. I don't remember what this gathering of the entire school was all about, possibly it was the singing of carols, with one or two other items by older scholars. I know that I was asked if I would sing the song again, for the benefit of everyone.

It was then that my courage failed me; I couldn't face the prospect of standing up before the whole school and, as an excuse, I told the teacher that I was sorry but I had forgotten the words of the song.

41

I'm sure he was far from convinced with my explanation, and I was made to realize what a poor excuse it was, when after the concert ended the teacher brought me my father's book containing the words of his songs - I had left it in my desk in the classroom. The teacher must have been well aware of the real reason why I had not accepted the opportunity of singing for the whole school - I had just lost my nerve.Speaking of 'nerves', I had never before been to a swimming baths when 'SWIMMING' appeared on the school curriculum, so this situation was about to change.

We had to walk up from school to the swimming baths at the top of Storr Hill, and at first I found the whole experience most disconcerting.

For a while, and until I got accustomed to it, I was petrified from the moment I stepped inside the door until I got back on to the pavement again. The sheer volume of noise, made by forty or fifty boys, I found quite alarming as it reverberated around the lofty hall, which was formerly a theatre - Ashington's Theatre, as my mother used to tell me.

To begin with, I wasn't at all happy at having to strip off and step under the shower, before entering the menacing depths of the shallow end of the bath - by means of the steps, whilst most of the other lads who possessed swimming costumes, simply jumped into the pool. I felt most conspicuous in a pair of borrowed football shorts. Since my parents hadn't thought it necessary to provide me with a proper swimming costume, I suppose I was facing an experience of which they had no knowledge; I'm sure that neither of them had ever been in a swimming pool, so neither of them had ever learnt to swim.

No wonder that I felt nervous about visiting the baths, for the first month or so, at any rate. William, on the other hand, had an elder brother from whom he was able to borrow a costume.

I don't think I learnt to swim more than a breadth of the pool while I was a pupil at Wyke, but later, swimming became one of the sports that I enjoyed immensely when I and a few friends used to attend the baths on Saturday mornings - just for pleasure. It was only then that I really learnt to swim, though actually I performed no better than to gain one or two Swimming Certificates.

My mind goes back to those days, when we lived, firstly in Fountain Street and then in Shaw Street, Moor Top. I always knew that, although not really amongst the noticeably poor, we hadn't a lot to go on with, but my parents made the best of what we had. My father was in full-time work, though he didn't earn a very big wage. Our life-style was fashioned to suit our circumstances

I recall now, though, that not only did we have enjoyable times around the piano, my father playing and singing ballads for practice, but I remember that later when my sister was growing up, there were other activities as well as singing around the piano, in which we all took part, and one of these activities was the making of tabbed rugs.

We possessed a rug-making frame of our own, which I suppose my parents had had made for them by a local joiner, or perhaps it was made by 'Uncle Charlie', the husband of my dad's cousin, where we went to spend a night at the time of the Low Moor Explosion.

I remember that this frame was in use quite frequently, in addition to being borrowed, just as frequently, by one neighbour or another.

Because my father was employed as a stuff warehouseman, it was quite a simple matter for him to acquire discarded ends of rolls of different kinds of cloth, such as serges, gabardines and similar good quality materials, which, when cut into strips of the correct length, made just the right sort of 'tabs', as they were known, for making rugs.

Canvas too, for attaching to the frame to make the backing for the rug, was also easily obtainable by my father from the department where he worked, because they used a great deal of it for packing pieces for both Home and Export trade.

It seemed that, in the business of rug-making, we were far better placed than many of our neighbours, since all the essential materials were so easily acquired.

In those days, during the war and also for a few years after the war, warmth and comfort in the home were amongst the important needs of most families, especially during winter-time. Coal was relatively cheap and plentiful, but wall-to-wall carpeting was very expensive and very rare in our neighbourhood, where most floors were covered with linoleum, on which were usually one or two tabbed rugs.

These rugs were of particular value where they were used on stone floors, because, being made largely of woollen materials, they were warm and comfortable, though it must be admitted that they did tend to collect grit and dirt from the street, and they were rather heavy for one person to take out of doors to be given a good shake.

I don't recall that my mother did a lot of knitting, and certainly I rarely saw her knitting stockings. I think that this was a skill that she never really acquired. It seemed to me then that this was an occupation for grandmothers, for I do remember that my grandmother used to knit grey woollen stockings, now and then. I did notice that the grandmothers of some of my friends often seemed to be knitting whenever I called at their homes

I noticed too, that most housewives who had families to care for, found it necessary to spend some part of each week darning stockings.

I recall that some women, especially grandmothers, used to make their knitting skills available for hire by putting announcements in shop windows which read - STOCKINGS RE-FOOTED. Presumably there were always customers for this kind of knitting service.

I never found out why stockings wore into holes so easily; but wear into holes they certainly did, especially children's stockings. It was quite usual, for instance, if one of your friends needed to take off his boots or shoes, for a bare heel or a couple of toes to be revealed. Of course that never, never happened to me!

Most of the houses that I visited, the homes of relatives or friends, were those of people whose circumstances were very similar to our own; that is to say, that while they were not 'well-off', they did manage to feed and clothe their families and furnish their homes in a modest fashion.

Many of the homes boasted a tall sideboard, as ours did, which was carefully dusted and polished before the week-end, and consequently, it was treated with a great deal of respect.

I don't think that the 3-piece suite had really made its appearance in those days, certainly not amongst working-class people such as ourselves, for the simple reason it seems to me, that our homes were generally too small to permit such extravagance, though sometimes a horse-hair settee provided seating for visitors, and occasionally a couple of matching chairs could be squeezed into the room, though none of the horse-hair-covered furniture was looked upon favourably by young lads with bare knees, who found worn horse-hair upholstery particularly irritating.

With a piano as well as a sideboard, we had little enough room at Fountain Street, and even when we moved to the larger house at Moor Top, it was some time before we managed a settee, with a couple of straight-backed chairs, upholstered in the same pattern of cut moquette, so we were moving up in the world. However, we did make room for Granddad's 'cratch', and a sprung rocking chair which had been passed on from I don't know where. We obviously hadn't a lot of space for indoor games.

The table-top was of plain white wood, and when it was being used for meals it was covered with a well-starched linen cloth. When the table was not being used for meals however, it was considered to be the centre-piece of the room, and it was covered with a maroon plush cover, with tassels all round the edge.

Our single, downstairs room had a high mantelpiece over the fireplace, which held various ornaments, usually printed in golden letters which announced 'A PRESENT FROM MORECAMBE', or from some other seaside resort. The mantelpiece was hung with a pelmet of the same material as the table-cover (if we were lucky.) and this too was hung with tassels.

If the sideboard was a piece of furniture to be treated with special respect (and it was) then it seemed that the same could be said of the table; in most houses the legs of the table were beautifully turned and french polished. There was every reason therefore, to protect those table legs from the kicks they received during the rush of a busy working (and playing) week, so they were covered with thick, black wool stockings.

I became aware of this custom when I was very young, though I'm sure I didn't understand the reason that lay behind it, and to tell the truth I don't think I'm a lot wiser now.

I do remember though, that if visitors were expected an Saturdays or Sundays, then the stockings came off, and the legs were exposed in all their nakedness. Perhaps this was the origin of another explanation for the covering of table legs, but I was unable, myself, to give much credence to the explanation.

It was said by an adult, not to me, but in my hearing I should add, that stockings were worn on table legs simply for reasons of modesty. It is a thought but no more than that, I think.

NINE

FOOTBALL AND HOCKEY STICKS

Living near to Harold Park as we did, it is quite understandable how many of my playing hours were spent there, many of them on the 'Rec', which was reasonably safe. It wasn't until I was much older and we had moved to Moor Top, that I was allowed extra freedom because the park lake was always a bit of a threat and a danger.

In summer, however, we spent a lot of time on the 'Rec'. There was plenty of grass surrounding the football pitch, and some shorter, younger grass on the pitch itself. Away from the pitch, the grass was always more plentiful with buttercups, daisies and dandelions in profusion.

On those lovely, warm summer days that we used to get so many more of in days gone by, there were always bees and butterflies to be chased, but why - I don't really know - perhaps it was just the joy of the chase. The possibility of being stung by a bee was always present, and perhaps an extra incentive to brave boys.

I have a vague recollection that we had been shown by older boys how to remove the stings from bees. This was cruel and resulted in the death of the bees, but sometimes they struck back and stung our fingers quite painfully, even through the material of the cap that we used with which to catch them. The slight risk involved made the chasing of bees more exciting than chasing butterflies.

After I had grown bigger and stronger, especially after we had moved to Moor Top, the 'Rec' offered other activities which began to claim my interest. I found, along with a few friends of my own age, that kicking a ball about was always a pleasure, and this led to my taking a boy's interest in a 'real' football team.

This meant, for me, 'Low Moor Hotspurs', who played their home games on the 'Rec'. I supported them by my occasional presence at their home games, but I don't think that my support was exactly vital to the team's existence; I did, however consider them to be 'MY TEAM'.

Another local football team whose name often cropped up in conversations was that of the 'Low Moor A.F.C.'. I never knew very much about them, and I don't think I cared very much either, for the reason that the boys who used to talk about them, were not close friends of mine. I think the team used to play on a pitch which was between Huddersfield Road and Cleckheaton Road, where the playing fields are now, but I'm not quite sure.

The Hotspurs played in red and white striped shirts and white shorts, which, if they had just been washed looked very smart. I probably saw the A.F.C. play only once, and I thought that their jerseys, which I think were black and white, were rather dull compared with those of the Hotspurs, so I stuck to 'MY' TEAM - 'LOW MOOR HOTSPURS'. In games of football with my mates. I was always a 'Hotspur', never an A.F.C.

I think it was after we had lived at Moor Top for a year or two that I, along with my friends, used to go to watch the games of football which were played in a field not very far away from our homes. These games were part of an Inter-works Competition.

The games were played on late summer evenings, on a pitch that had been prepared just a field-length away from the footpath which ran past Scott's farm, but I think that the football field was probably part of Dyson's Seed Farm.

We used to talk very knowingly about the 'INTER-WORKS', though I don't believe that at the time I, for one, had the slightest idea what the term meant. We found these games interesting, but whether it was entirely because of our love of the game, or because there was always the possibility that after half-time we might be given a drink of left-over coffee, which, hopefully contained a drop of rum.

I remember an occasion when one of the players had the misfortune to break a leg in a tackle. Now that was interesting. The unfortunate lad was loaded on to an old door and carried by about four men, all the way down to Abb Scott Lane, where an ambulance took him away to hospital.

I remember too, another match in which a cousin of mine, Frank Metcalfe from Storr Hill, was a member of a team representing Buttershaw Mills, where he worked as an engineer.

47

Between Moor Top and Royds Hall there were fields all around us where cattle grazed and where there were attractive woods and copses which we made full use of, especially in spring and summer. Even in winter there were lots of meadows with frozen ponds on which we made slides, to give us an hour's enjoyment on moonlit evenings.

We used to spend a lot of our leisure time in and around the fields in this area, and the strange thing was that I don't remember ever being chased off the land, or shouted at by the farmers, for being there. I certainly never remember seeing notices which said 'TRESPASSERS WILL BE PROSECUTED' - happy, happy days.

Just about where the Alms Houses are now there was a lane (Seed Lane?) which gave access to all these fields, but more directly to the farms occupied by the Scotts and the Dysons; this last was later farmed by the Hughes brothers until they had to vacate the farm to make way for the new estate.

The track leading to Scott's farm went straight forward from Abb Scott Lane, but apart from its importance in this connection, it was little used, except, perhaps by fishermen who used to approach the Royds Hall dam from that side.

Just a few yards along this access lane, a footpath led past Scott's farm by way of a stile, and then the path led through the fields and up the hill to emerge next to the cottages in Royds Hall Lane. These cottages were, and still are, opposite to the entrance to the Hall.

From our part of Low Moor, this was the quickest and most pleasant way to the Low Moor Cricket Club's ground, to Judy Woods and to Norwood Green, all popular places for walks and picnics.

Royds Hall Lane then continued past the cricket field and, turning right between the cricket field and the edge of Judy Woods and then lower down it turned sharply left until it reached High Fernley Road, where a signpost indicated (somewhat surprisingly) that this was the furthest point of Royds Hall Lane.

Just a few yards from the beginning of the track in Abb Scott Lane, another track turned sharp right in the direction of Buttershaw. This lane or track was chiefly used as the access road for Seed Farm.

At the farm entrance was a row of cottages, where I think the Hughes brothers with their wives lived, in the two cottages furthest from the entrance. Next to them lived the farm worker whose name was Wilfred with his wife, who I believe was the daughter of the elder of the Hughes brothers.

In the first cottage lived a friend of my sister - Phyllis Briggs, her brother and their parents. I was not aware that there was any family connection between the Briggs and the Hughes families.

Part of the field below the cottages had been fenced off to allow a lawn to be laid for a tennis court. I spent some very happy hours playing on this court, after it had been rented by young people from School Street Primitive Methodist Church, and it was there that I learnt to play tennis.

A short distance from the farm entrance the track joined Royds Hall Lane, after which it carried on across the lane as little more than a footpath which carried on past a large mound surmounted by an air shaft, the purpose of which I never really knew, but it was probably connected with one of the many small coal pits that used to abound in the area. This path finally joined Pit Lane, which came down from Halifax Road.

I confess that I find it rather difficult now, to remember where all the tracks and footpaths in the area led, but they all had served various pits and farms at one time.

One trusts that the massive take-over of good farm land was absolutely essential, in the interest of securing proper housing for so many of Bradford's citizens, who were often bringing up young families in the midst of worn-out sewage systems and overcrowded living conditions.

The re-housing of so many people has meant, unfortunately, that all these sites have lost their identities, and for people of my generation,(for whom those sites gave so much pleasure), they are sometimes recalled as happy memories, though increasingly only with difficulty.

My thoughts now return once again to Low Moor, and to the personalities I knew when I was growing up there.

It occurs to me that there must be few people still living in Low Moor who used to attend the Sunday School at the 'Prims', who do not remember Miss Baxter with affection.

Miss Mary Ann Baxter is remembered by a decreasing number of us as being a commanding personality whose influence on the children attending the Sunday School was quite impressive.

She had a regal bearing, with a quiet, cultured voice, and she had only to walk into a room where the children were having a lesson, for her presence to be felt at once by everyone, and a kind of awe descended upon both teachers and scholars. Where, one is tempted to ask, are such influential characters to be found today?

If she conveyed the impression of belonging to a different social class, then I am sure that this was quite unintentional and simply the result of good breeding and a standard of education that our parents had been unable to afford.

She was well known in the Great Horton Primitive Methodist Circuit (to which the School Street Chapel belonged) as an indefatigable worker for the Circuit, for the Missionary cause, and for her Sunday School activities at Low Moor, where she was a Superintendent for many years. She was ably supported by her niece May, who lived with her, and who also had quite an influence upon young people in the Sunday School.

Reflecting upon the influence of Miss Baxter and May, reminded me of the fact that, with the help of her uncle Irvine Shaw, the husband of Miss Baxter's sister, May, started a hockey team for the young ladies of the Sunday School. A field was rented behind Carter Fold, goal posts were erected and the field prepared for play. I can't remember very much about their fortunes in this field (sic), but I suspect that success against any kind of opposition was little more than a dream.

There may have been a few of the young ladies with a little aptitude for the game, but amongst the remainder were such unlikely aspirants as my Aunt Carrie, who, I am sure, had never wielded a hockey stick in her life, and Menetta Couble (later to become Mrs Arthur Woodhead) who was equally inexperienced.

I don't remember that the enterprise ever really took off and, if I remember correctly, it wasn't long before it became little more than a memory.

Following this slight diversion, I now return to the subject of home, and the duties to which my mother adhered quite strictly.

With the arrival of electricity into our homes, the way was slowly being opened up for a much easier and healthier life-style, but Mondays, like the law of the Medes and Persians, was unalterable - Monday was 'WASHING DAY'.

On a 'GOOD' washing day, when there was a nice breeze, and when the sun was shining brightly so as to dry the clothes quickly, as they hung on lines stretched across the street, my mother might get her washing finished in one day and even start to iron a few things before dad arrived home from work. That was when the electric iron came into its own.

A 'POOR' washing day, which was often, but not always, in winter-time, was a day when there were numerous showers, causing my mother to have to dash out into the street to bring in her clothes from the line and into the house, to prevent them getting wet, and pegging them all out again when the rain stopped.

When the wet clothes were brought indoors, if the weather looked unpromising they were often hung on a creel above the fireplace, or on a clothes horse in front of the fire. I still recall that, as a child it wasn't much fun for me to have to stay indoors on a wet washing day, with a blazing fire hidden by wet clothes from which steam slowly arose. Needless to say, it wasn't much fun for my mother either.

Wet Mondays were not very enjoyable for either of us and very tiring for my mother. Most of the children on the street realised that wet Mondays were the days when mothers never had a great deal of patience with their children, especially during holidays.

With a young family to look after, in common with many of her neighbours, my mother must have been extremely tired before the end of a busy day. I distinctly remember an occasion when I was quite young, hearing a quiet cry for help - 'O Lord help me.' escape her lips, but she never allowed me to hear such cries for relief when I was older.

In such a small house as ours, wet Mondays meant that almost the whole of the play space was taken up by wet or drying clothes, so what could a small boy do? The only alternative was to play in the 'chamber steps', throwing a soft ball to the top of the stairs, and then trying to catch it as it bounced back down the steps, the sound of which, my mother found somewhat irritating after an hour or so. The other alternative was to play in the bedroom, and on my own that was not much fun.

I remember when we were living in Shaw Street at Moor Top, my parents bedroom had a fireplace, and if I was not very well I was put into their bed, for ease of communication, because it was nearest to the stairs steps. At such times, I was often accompanied by a glazed earthenware bedwarmer, which was rather like a heavy, brown pipe which had been heated in the oven and then wrapped in a piece of blanket.

This was, presumably, the basic piece of equipment for us in cases of children's illnesses, though I recall that later we had a more popular type of stone(?) hot water bottle which, when filled with boiling water and wrapped in a piece of blanket would keep warm for an hour or so.

What I liked best though when I was sick, was when the fireplace was brought into use. My dad used to bring up shovelful of glowing coals from the fireplace downstairs, thus providing an instant fire to warm the bedroom. In these circumstances, when I was put into my parents bed on dark Winter days, I enjoyed the experience very much as I lay there watching the play of the shadows thrown by the flames on to the ceiling.

When my sister and I were getting older and both attending school, I believe that my mother did find life a little easier and I think she did find time, in the midst of an active life, to have a little leisure. This was indicated by the fact that made the opportunity to go the Women's Meeting down at the chapel, on a Tuesday afternoon. I believe that, along with some of our neighbours, she enjoyed this weekly break.

The women's meeting, or more correctly, The Women's Devotional Hour, was well attended, no doubt because of the fact that it regularly brought a lot of hard-working housewives together, with an opportunity to sing and talk about their faith as well as giving them a chance to share each other's problems.

I have no doubt though that, after the heavy day my mother had had on a Monday, Tuesday would be a more relaxed sort of day, but even then she would be kept busy, with meals to prepare and other duties to be done, such as stockings to darn and other mending jobs.

TEN

WOMEN'S WORK IS NEVER DONE

When we were living in Fountain Street, I am certain that we had no such thing as a vacuum cleaner, even of the non-electric type, until long after we had moved to Moor Top. What we did have, however, and what many working-class people like ourselves had, was an 'EWBANK' carpet sweeper, and what an invaluable implement it was for keeping carpets free from dust and dirt.

Once in a while, carpets and mats were taken up and hung on a line across the street,(provided that no-one had washing out at the time.) and given a good beating with a carpet beater made specially for the job, from cane or bamboo.

Rugs needed to be shaken by two people, usually Mother and Dad, taking the corners of the rug in each hand and, bringing their hands together, throwing the rug into the air, at the same time spreading their arms out as wide as possible in order to produce a loud cracking sound. I liked that. This technique was guaranteed to shake out most of the dust and grit from the rug.

I am certain that my Mother was no exception amongst the householders of Fountain Street as regards the pride that she took in keeping her home clean, both inside and out.

Though none of the houses on the street possessed a garden, the occupants were just as concerned about the outside of their homes as they were about the insides. To justify this point of view, I think it was my Mother who was once heard to say in my hearing 'Ah well, there are more passers-by than callers-in.' I don't think anyone could argue with that philosophy.

As a consequence of this dedication to the presenting of a clean approach to one's door, the steps and the flagstones in front of the house were swept and 'swilled' regularly, after which the edges of the steps were picked out with white or yellow scouring stone.

One of the contributing causes of dust and dirt on the pavement was the fact that each house needed to have regular deliveries of coal or coke which, even when delivered in bags, made a certain amount of dirt on the flags when the coal was tipped through the cellar grate.

Sometimes (when we could afford it,) we would have a ton of coal delivered in the specially designed coal carts with very high, outward-sloping sides. These were always readily recognisable on the streets of Low Moor.

When these deliveries were made we had, obviously, a lot more dirt on the pavement than we had with bags, because the coal was tipped on to the pavement in front of the house, for the householder to shovel through the cellar grate. Afterwards, it was more than ever necessary to 'Swill down' the flags with hot soapy water and a stiff 'besom' brush.

This procedure was not only so that the pavement in front of the house looked nice and clean again, but also because the task of swilling the dirt away prevented any callers from 'trailing' the dirt inside the house on their boots and shoes.

All the women on the street, or so it seemed to me, showed the same desire for cleanliness, and this was seen in their disposition to keep their windows clean and sparkling - even the bedroom windows.

I don't remember that we ever had a window cleaner when we lived on Fountain Street, and it was quite a common sight to see a neighbour, or my Mother for that matter, seated on the upstairs window- sill, with her legs inside the bedroom, the lower half of the window having been raised to enable her to put her head and shoulders through the open space, and then lowering the window on to her thighs. By raising and lowering each half of the sash windows it was a fairly easy operation to clean the outside of the bedroom windows, without calling upon the services of the window cleaner, although it looked a rather more risky operation than it actually was.

I don't seem able to recall exactly what routine was followed by my Mother with regard to household duties, but it seems fairly logical to assume that the major cleaning operations, both inside and outside the house, were carried out towards the week-end, perhaps on a Friday, since I seem to remember quite well that Thursday was 'Baking Day', so Friday was quite possibly the day for 'Blackleading' and associated jobs.

In winter time, especially after a week of roaring fires, the old-style range looked in need of some restoration by way of a good cleaning and polishing. That was the time when my Mother produced the dirty old basket which contained the black-lead and the various brushes, as well as a pair of dirty old gloves. Unless I am quite mistaken, the magic black-lead polish was called 'ZEBO'. When this liquid was applied to the iron grate and to the 'end-irons', after a vigorous brushing, the resulting shine added a brightness to the whole room.

Thursday I remember well as being 'Baking Day'. Following breakfast my Mother would clear the table, and after giving it a good wipe-over would then place upon it all the ingredients needed for the weekly bake; then she would produce from somewhere, a white wood baking board, and put that on the table too.

The next step was to bring up from the cellar the all-important baking bowl. This, of course, was the largest bowl in the house as it had to be, in order to accommodate the ingredients for a week's supply of bread for the family. The bowl was then placed on its side in front of the fire, in order that it should be warmed thoroughly before my Mother started the baking process.

I am not sure, but possibly all family-sized baking bowls looked exactly the same as ours and made from red clay with yellow glazing on the inside. It had straight, outward-sloping sides and quite a small base, which design was no doubt to assist the kneading operation.

From the age of about three I was captivated by the whole process of bread making. As I remember it, Mother used to put some warm milk (or was it milk and water?) in a jug or a pint pot and then crumbled it into the required amount of yeast, gently beating the mixture into a paste.

The next step, as I recall (and these are definitely NOT instructions on how to make bread) was to take the flour - half-a-stone, or even a stone, depending on how many loaves were required at the time, emptying the bag into the warmed baking bowl, and adding the baking powder. Then came the really intriguing bit, for me.

At this point, Mother would scoop out from the middle of the bowl of flour a handful or perhaps several handfuls, so as to make a large hole, into which she poured the yeast liquid. Then began the really hard work.

Starting at the hole in the middle, Mother used to work her hands round and round the hole, gradually working more flour into the mixture as the dough became stiffer and stiffer and more difficult to work, when a drop more of the warm milk was added, until it became one large lump of dough. This large lump was then thumped and pounded with her fists and slapped against the sides of the bowl, making a cracking sound which I just loved to hear. This thumping and pounding of the dough continued until, eventually either the dough or my Mother could take no more.

The bowl containing the dough was next placed in front of the fire for the dough to 'rise', after which there was more thumping for a while. When my Mother judged that the time was right, the scales with the pyramid of brass weights were brought to the table,the loaf tins were smeared with lard, and the baking board was placed on the table and sprinkled with flour.

When the dough had 'risen' sufficiently, Mother took a carving knife and cut off a large piece of it and weighed it to see if there was too much or if a little more was required. When she was satisfied, the lump of dough was placed on the floured baking board and roughly patted into shape, after which it was placed, quite carefully, it seemed to me, into the greased loaf tin. This process was repeated until the required number of tins were in the oven and the baking of the bread began.

This was roughly what happened on a 'Good Baking Day'. On a 'Poor Baking Day', oh dear. That was a day when nothing seemed to go right, and my Mother's patience was sorely tried. A day when the oven simply would not 'Draw'. This sometimes happened on damp, still days when there was no breeze at all and when a draught was sorely needed to get the oven really hot, and when a little help from a pair of bellows didn't achieve the desired effect.

When Dad came home from work, Mother would pour out the story of the struggle she had had trying to get the oven heating satisfactorily. His eventual response was to put a firework under the oven, in the hope that the minor explosion would be sufficient to shift any soot that had collected in a vital area. We used to keep one or two 'crackers' just for such an emergency. They were called 'Squibs', I think.

Letting off a squib was sometimes all that was required to shift the soot and enable the oven to perform satisfactorily, which did a great deal for Mother's peace of mind.

Draughts around the house were always annoying, especially for older people, who sometimes had to resort to curtains and screens, in order to divert various draughts from a much-loved corner of the house. where, for example, the 'cratch' or the rocking chair was usually to be found.

There were times however, when draughts were considered to be something of a boon, as well as when there was baking to be done. I discovered that another occasion when a decent draught was important was on the day when ironing was to be done. Everyone knows that irons weren't always the efficient instruments that they are today, and some of the early irons that I recall were, to say the least, somewhat primitive.

The first iron that I remember seeing in use was a charcoal-burning iron, and I recall that my Mother sometimes had quite a struggle to get the charcoal lighted, and even then it failed to burn as brightly as she would have liked. At such times she would stand the iron outside the door, on the step, 'to catch the draught'. This would generally be sufficient to cause the charcoal to burn brightly and so heat the iron. I remember the charcoal irons especially, firstly because they had a little doorway at the back where the charcoal was inserted, and secondly because they had a very noticeable feature in the form of a small chimney from which wisps of smoke used to curl when the iron was in use.

There were also the 'flat irons', which were very widely used. These were put straight on to the fire or on a gas ring to heat. It was normal to have a couple of these in use at the same time, so that while one was being used for ironing, the other was being heated.

I was always impressed by the use of a 'slipper' on these irons. The 'slipper' was a flat, shiny metal shoe which clipped on to the iron, after it had been taken from the fire and wiped free of ash. The slipper always provided a good, clean surface which glided easily over the item being ironed.

Another activity which has not survived the electrical revolution which took place in the home, was the toasting of bread. My grandparents had a toasting fork which always hung beside the fireplace. It was a three-pronged utensil, mostly of brass, but with one middle prong of iron, I believe.

It was good on a cold, winter evening to be able to sit in front of a good fire, holding out a fork with a slice of bread or half a current teacake for toasting. It was a very pleasant way either of getting warm after coming in from outside, or for keeping warm.

Who would deny, however, that the convenience of the electric toaster has considerable merits? I recall that Granddad's toasting fork became my parents' property, but what eventually happened to it, I have no idea.

ELEVEN

THE LOW MOOR COMPANY

I am glad now, that I grew up in Low Moor before the last traces of its former importance as a coal and iron-producing area had given way to the manufacture of steel. The pride of Low Moor - the giant steam hammer and the blast furnaces were removed and taken to Sheffield, by the Thos. Ward Company.

I recall with pleasure a school visit, when a number of scholars from Grange Road were taken around all the various iron and coke-making plants - it was a wonderful experience, especially for a local lad who heard these activities spoken of almost daily.

When we lived in Shaw Street, Moor Top, straight opposite our house were the backs of the houses, the fronts of which were in Cemetery Road (as they still are). I remember that Tom Wormald, with his wife and daughter lived in one of those houses, next to William Stobart's uncle - Herbert Barraclough and his family.

Both these men worked for the Low Moor Company, in different capacities. Herbert Barraclough was, I think, a bookkeeper in the offices at Low Moor while Tom Wormald was a Pit Steward. I didn't exactly know where he worked, which is not really surprising as I was only about six or seven years of age at the time. I just know that he had a job of some responsibility at a colliery, and this was probably the one at Norwood Green.

He used to ride to work every day on what we used to call a 'sit-up-and-beg' type of bicycle, and I remember that he always mounted the cycle from the back, by putting his left foot on the back-step and then moving forward on to the saddle, after a push-off with his right foot. This method of mounting a bicycle must have died out when they ceased to be fitted with a back-step.

The pit at Norwood Green was the last working pit that I can remember, but there must have been several hundred pits within a radius of ten miles of the Low Moor Company's Works, though many of them were quite small 'Open Cast' mines and 'Day Holes'. Together with the larger pits however, they were capable of producing a phenomenal quantity of the good quality 'Better Bed' and 'Black Bed' coal needed by local industry and by the householders of the area.

James Parker recorded in his '30 Villages' that the annual output of the Low Moor Company's pits in 1903 was about 420,000 tons, a quantity of which was used for iron making and the rest used either for steam raising or for sale locally as well as for large users of coal further afield.

One cannot fail to be impressed by the fact that almost every engraving which depicts the Low Moor Ironworks in its heyday, offers some advice of the extent to which coal was used, from the forest of chimneys to be seen belching out thick black smoke.

The mining of 420,000 tons of coal annually represents a lot of coal by any standards and by my reckoning this amounts to more than 1,100 tons of coal EVERY WORKING DAY.

Obviously, a lot of horse-power was required to shift that amount of coal, some of which was carried on the various rail-roads throughout the district, to the staiths and other collecting points. It also meant that a lot of coal carts and wagons were required, so there was a great need for repair shops such as the 'Wrights' or 'Reights' shop at the bottom of Abb Scott Lane where my grandfather used to work as a farrier and blacksmith. It was there that so many of the company's horses went to be shod, and where the coal carts went to be repaired.

From 1903 onwards, it seems clear that the number of pits in use fell somewhat rapidly as the seams of coal became exhausted. Although there is now little evidence of what were once very active pits, here and there can be seen on an up to date map of the area, the name of a road or street which is a reminder of the activity which once took place thereabouts.

In what is now the Carr House Gate area there were, years ago, working pits with such names as Hill Lands Pit, Ruffield Side Pit and Milner Ing Pit, to name just a few. These names have been retained on the Delf Hill Estate, whilst in the Low Moor (or Hill Top) areas there were the pits at Hill Stones and Fiddler Hill, as well as a number of others.

In her book 'Low Moor - the story of a village' - Mrs Constance Myers records the fact that trucks used to run on rails from the New Biggin, where the blast furnaces were, tipping their loads of hot slag from the 'Arches', at the point where the arches crossed Brighouse Road.

I remember seeing these large, glowing tips, which were particularly noticeable at night time. These tips, of course, disappeared when the arches were demolished, the slag from the tips being carted away for road making.

What evidence there was around Low Moor in my boyhood days, and which still remains in a very few cases, suggests that there were many places throughout the district that were used for tipping slag and scale from the Low Moor Company's furnaces and pits.

I have memories of spending many happy hours playing on the red scale hill which used to exist where part of the Horsfall Playing Fields were laid out, towards the Hill Stones end.

As lads, most of us found this area an adventure playground, due to its rock like formations, with the appearance of having been welded together while still hot. This huge pile, according to my recollections, was composed almost entirely of red scale, and this became quite useful years later, when it was used in the construction of the new road - Woodside Road - from Low Moor to Wyke, about the year 1928, I think it was.

Near the top of Fiddler Hill, or Union Road as it is today, there was another huge tip. This was behind Brunswick House and it was of a quite different material. Possibly it was the tip used for disposing of the waste from the Fiddler Hill or Hill Stones Pits, which were located thereabouts. In this case, the scale was black, so not surprisingly, the tip was known to us as 'The Black Hill'.

We used to play a great deal on the Black Hill and I must say that we were able to enjoy ourselves without at any time being sent off, either by Alderman William Warburton of Brunswick Cottage, or by Walter Bowler of Brunswick House.

I remember an occasion when I was playing in the fields at the back of the Black Hill. Unless I am mistaken, that particular field is still preserved as an open space.

My companion on this occasion was Wilfred Illingworth, whose father, Inspector Illingworth, was based at the Low Moor Police Station. Inspector Illingworth, Mrs Illingworth and their three boys, of whom Wilfred was the youngest, lived in the house attached to the Police Station in Common Road.

Hill Stones was another of those areas which must have seen many different activities over the years. This was the name of the small, hilly area which was no doubt a disused quarry, at the top of Park Road, beyond which there was just a footpath through to Halifax Road.

I remember that there were a number of very large earth fast boulders, and amongst those boulders were areas where all kinds of slag had been tipped in years gone by. I am sure that I remember the remains of a barn and some stables at the very top of the hill too.

Concerning the time when Wilfred and I were up in the field. I can't really remember why we were there, perhaps he had been asked to deliver a message to a man who was mowing the field with a horse and a mowing machine. At any rate, it came on to rain rather heavily and the three of us stood against the horses's side, with a couple of horse blankets over our heads, sheltering from the rain.

Now why, after all these years (more than 70), should I remember the name of the man with a horse and a mowing machine, I simply cannot imagine? But I remember quite distinctly that his name was Will Gascoigne. Not Bill or Willie, you will notice - but Will. If my memory is to be relied upon, I think he was the brother or cousin of Mrs Illingworth.

All this area was cleared of the rocks and scale when the building programme for the St Abbs Estate got under way, so that nowadays any evidence of the former use of the land is almost impossible to find.

At the top on Union Road, it is possible that there was a pit near Collier Gate, not far from the group of houses there, which I remember were called 'Saunders Nook'. These houses were probably built by the Low Moor Company, to house the colliers who worked at the Saunders Nook Pit. If these assumptions are correct, it does seem likely that somewhere in the vicinity of the pit was a coal staith which would be known as the Collier Gate Staith.

James Parker records that as far back as 1780 'Iron Roads' or rail tracks were laid to facilitate the transport of coal from the many pits in the district, to the Iron Works, and to the staiths in the Wibsey and Hill Top areas. Rails were also laid to carry coal from Low Moor to a staith in Bradford also known as 'Collier Gate Staith', which was situated on the site of a former Police Station in Swaine Street.

I remember that, as lads, (although we didn't always know what we were talking about) we did sometimes refer to the 'Iron Roads', because older people spoke about these places in our hearing. I believe that we referred frequently in this manner to the track which ran along the bottom of Royds Hall Dam, through the trees, to emerge in Abb Scott Lane, and I expect the track can still be seen.

A lot of coal was sold in the vicinity of the staith at Low Moor, perhaps to householders and merchants, as well as to coal using mills and factories. Thousands of tons were, however, shipped by way of the Old Bradford Canal, which was easily accessible in the days of the Low Moor Company.

According to James Parker the following were the 'Iron Roads' in existence in 1852:-

1st   The Low Moor Company had a coal staith near to the Old Black Horse, Little Horton

2nd   Another, near to Briggella Mills, from which point the coal was distributed locally.

3rd   To the Low Moor Works, from their various Ironstone and Coal Pits.

4th   To Bierley Iron Works

5th   Previous to 1849, to Shelf Iron Works

There seems to be little doubt that the Low Moor Company's staith in Bradford, which extended from Collier Gate to Well Street was, in the middle of the nineteenth century, a very large undertaking indeed.

Naturally, it took a few years for me to assimilate the facts concerning Low Moor's past. It was after we had moved to Moor Top and when I was growing up, that I began to develop an awareness of the past and, without realising this at the time, I was actually moving amongst the pages of history.

This was the period when I began to become aware of residences such as Royds Hall for example, being spoken of with a sort of veneration which was new to me, as being a place of historic interest.

Although at first this new awareness didn't make a great impression upon me, I gradually came to understand a little more about Low Moor's past and I started to acquire an interest in it.

This interest was furthered quite considerably, by my reading of Parker's book - '30 Villages from Hipperholme to Tong' which, as I have already said, was given to my father by Alderman William Warburton, a long time ago. I was about eight years old when I began to explore the book, but it was many years before I grew fond of it. I did however, dip into the book from time to time; using it more as a reference book than as a book to sit down and read, but as a result some of the details stayed in my mind.

The part played by the Low Moor Company in the development of Low Moor, together with the company's concern for the welfare of its workers, can hardly be over estimated. These facts are important if one pays due regard to the general standard of living which was the norm when the company began its operations.

It cannot be allowed to pass without comment that one of the most influential partners in the original conception of the Low Moor Ironworks, was the Rev Joseph Dawson, Minister of the Old Independent Chapel at Idle.

His knowledge of minerals was, according to James Parker, superior to that of any of his colleagues.

No doubt it was largely due to his influence that the moral aspects involved in becoming (and quite rapidly) large employers of labour, were not overlooked.

As more and more men were able to obtain employment at the ironworks, at the blast furnaces and in the local collieries, so more and more houses were required to accommodate their families.

Many people will, with good reason, look upon Low Moor nowadays (1995) as being a very dull place, but it was not always considered in such terms. It is without question that, when the Low Moor Company was great, and at its most influential - during the latter part of the nineteenth century and the first part of the twentieth - then Low Moor was prosperous too, and full of opportunity for the small businessman such as the butcher, the baker, the publican and so on.

The men who were employed at the collieries, at the ironworks, the blast furnaces and on the railways, as well as the women who worked in the mills, all ensured that during those years the name of Low Moor was synonymous with hard work and good products. These were the standards that helped to bring about full employment and ensured that the name Low Moor was one to be respected.

TWELVE

LOW MOOR WELCOMES JOHN WESLEY

Perhaps by today's standards wages were low, but they seem to have been sufficient to allow the men who flocked to Low Moor to earn some sort of a living, and to be able in most cases, to bring up quite large families.

It was not long, therefore, after the Low Moor Company began its operations - in 1790/91 - that mainly through the influence of the Rev. Joseph Dawson, a Day School and Sunday School was started in some converted buildings, later to be known as School Fold in Abb Scott Lane. The aim was to keep the boys off the streets and at the same time, with the help of the newly formed Wesleyan Society, to give them a rudimentary education, together with some teaching of Christian values.

The School was well attended, which says much for the devoted work of the teachers and for the kind of instruction that was made available. Eventually a stage was reached where there were more pupils seeking places than the little school was able to provide.

Most boys were apprentices with the Low Moor Company, and within a year or two of the school being founded, the company took over the King's Head (or Buttershaw House as it was originally known). The land adjoining was then farmed for the benefit of the apprentices, who were housed, fed and clothed there, as can be seen from the details of an account dated August 23rd 1794:-

William Bastow

	£	s	d
For Lads' meat and clothes			
at Buttershaw House	1	8	6

Mr Bastow was the man responsible for seeing that the lads were fed, clothed and educated, all at the Low Moor Company's expense.

From about the year 1798, the cottages in School Fold were often used by the growing Wesleyan movement, as one of a number of 'Preaching Places' in various parts of the district, until they were able to build their first chapel in 1809, not without much effort and self-sacrifice on the part of the members.

Assisted by the Low Moor Company, they were able, in 1838, to add a burial ground adjoining the church premises, and this was further enlarged in 1877.

It is perhaps worthy of mention that the plans for this first Wesleyan Chapel, in Wesley Place, Low Moor were prepared by Thos. Woodcock, the designer of the Low Moor Blast Furnaces.

The Low Moor Company continued to be involved supporting various benevolent activities in the area, such as housing and educational projects. One such project was the school associated with Holy Trinity Church, and which became known as Scott's School, being so called for many years because of the long and devoted service given by two of its first headmasters - Mr John Scott, who served for forty-four years, to be succeeded by his son, who served for eighteen years.

Scott's School was built by the Low Moor Company in 1814 and my father, was a pupil there when he was about five or six years of age, which would be around 1890.

I have some very happy memories of taking part in a production of 'The Pirates of Penzance' at the Central School (to give it its proper title), and this was probably in the early thirties.

The names of many of the people who were involved in this production come readily to mind, such as conductor John Bentley and accompanist Eddie Richmond. Hilda Bessie Priestley (to give her full maiden name) sang the principal role of Mabel, opposite George Carter (who married Bessie) as the Major General, Fred Proudler as the Pirate King, Annie Brown as Ruth, Norman Cooper as the Police Sergeant and Alfred Terry as Samuel.

I still remember the names of one or two members of the chorus such as Irvine Barraclough, for instance, who took me along for the first time , and Ben Hobson who I still meet regularly. Many other members of the chorus are, sadly, no longer with us.

Great days, in spite of the fact that I think that I was probably unemployed at the time!

Scott's School, that old building of many happy memories, and probably many sad ones too, is still standing, though no longer in use either as a Day School or as a Sunday School.

Many of the cottages which were erected by the Low Moor Company in different parts of Low Moor, continued to be occupied until the area, roughly between Old Hill Top and Park Road, was demolished and replaced by new houses and flats built for rent, by the Council and British Legion, as well as a number of houses that were built for sale. As a result of this re-building programme the whole area was transformed.

One remembers for example, some of those rows of old cottages in Manor Row, Colliergate, Lower School Street and New Street. When I was a young lad I often heard New Street referred to by ageing locals 't' Leather Pipe Row'.

It appears that there was time, only remembered by very few, when water was supplied to these cottages by means of a leather pipe instead of the normal method of underground pipes. I don't suppose that this method of distributing supplies of domestic water lasted very long, but the name was kept in mind by old residents for a long time afterwards.

Whilst it is probably true to say that most of the small cottages in the Low Moor district were built by the Low Moor Company to house their workpeople, it has to be said that the company was also responsible for building, for their directors and managers, quite a number of larger and more impressive residences, many of which have survived and have been occupied without a break to the present time.

Before going on to discuss some of the larger houses provided by the Low Moor Company, and to a lesser extent, by the Victoria Mills Company, I want to refer again to the group of cottages next to the timber yard at the bottom of Abb Scott Lane, where my father used to live at one time before he was married.

I notice that Mrs Myers in her book, pays particular attention to the local pronunciation of 'Reight's Shop'. I had always assumed, rightly or wrongly, this pronunciation was a local use of the shortened version of 'Wheelwright's Shop', for that is what it most certainly was at the time that my grandfather was employed there.

Those cottages, which at one time were together known as 'Carter Fold', were apparently built as shops by the Low Moor Company, from which their workpeople were supplied with provisions, in lieu of wages.

It is said that the bottom cottage, the one nearest to the timber yard, was a grocer's, the middle one a baker's and the uppermost was a butcher's. It is recorded that there used to be a slaughterhouse attached, although that feature disappeared many years ago, and I never heard any mention of it from either my father or my grandfather.

Whilst most of these interesting details are long forgotten, some members of today's generation keep in mind the many different phases through which this particular area has passed during the last two hundred years or so.

All true Methodists, (and no doubt a lot of Anglicans as well,) remember with some pride that it was here, in Carter Fold, on the 27th April 1747, that the founder of Methodism - John Wesley - preached on the Green adjoining Carter Fold, at the invitation of Betty Firth, the niece and housekeeper to Matthew Sugden, a tenant of one of the cottages in Carter Fold, which was at the time part of the Royds Hall Estate owned by Squire Leeds, of the Rookes family.

John Nelson, the stone mason from Birstall, and one of John Wesley's most famous preachers, visited Low Moor regularly and preached both indoors, in the home of Matthew Sugden, and also in the open air.

It does seem though, that whilst Squire Leeds, in no sense a religious man, was opposed to Nelson being invited to preach in the cottage occupied by one of his tenants, nevertheless, after actually hearing John Nelson preach, Leedes was so pleased with what he saw and heard as to befriend the mason-preacher ever after!

It is well known that because of his preaching, John Nelson suffered imprisonment in the vilest of dungeons beneath a butcher's shop at the top of Ivegate, in Bradford.

Betty Firth, mentioned above, married Thomas Worsnop, and he with George Hoyle of Raw Nook, were among the early supporters of Wesley and Nelson and became leaders of the little, but growing society at Low Moor; George Hoyle's home being used regularly as a 'Preaching Place', by itinerant preachers.

The story of Methodism, in the first half of the nineteenth century was said to be one of 'Success', though 'Progress' might best describe what was taking place. In spite of the loss around 1850, of 100,000 members to the Wesleyan Reformers, who wanted more Independence for each circuit, and more control for laymen over their own chapel affairs, Methodism continued to look and move forward in faith.

In 1801 the Wesleyan Methodist membership totalled 90,000, but fifty years later that total had increased to 358,000. The Primitive Methodists had increased their numbers from 200 in 1811 to 106,000 in 1851!

Just like their supporters, the growing Churches -, the Church of England on the one hand and the Wesleyans on the other - had to face many problems; problems of doctrine and of government. Concerning this situation Anthony Armstrong wrote :-

'Church and Chapel had one positive
solution to the problems of the time:
to provide more Churches and more Chapels,
as others were providing more drains,
more workhouses and every other kind of social utility'.

However, I must not pursue this line of thought any further. My story is mainly about life in Low Moor, so this is not the place to discuss at length the welfare of the Christian Church, either locally or nationally.

Between those two historic groups of houses - Carter Fold and School Fold - there are several other groups of old and interesting houses, the first of which is Moorside Farmhouse, separated from Carter Fold by several fields; I remember that there was a cart track (or was it one of the old Iron Roads?) which crossed the fields just below the dam, emerging from the coppice near the bottom of the drive up to Royds Hall, and just above the vicarage.

The farm used to be occupied by Isaac Brear, whom I remember as a typical rugged, fresh-faced farmer. He and his wife had one daughter, I believe, and she was a friend of my sister at one period. Isaac Brear was a dairy farmer, but whether he had a milk round himself, or whether he sold his milk to other milk roundsmen, I cannot now remember.

I do recall that Mrs Brear used to make butter, and there was an occasion when my sister came home from the farm with a half pound or so of butter, which Mrs Brear had sent us. I recall that it was, to me, quite different from the yellow butter we used to buy at the Co-op, because of its creamy-white colour, and also because of its pleasant, salty taste.

The next interesting house up Abb Scott Lane, is the one called Mineral House which was built by the Low Moor Company for its Mining Engineer. It appears to have undergone a number of modifications over the years, and when I was a boy I found the house somehow quite mysterious, as well as different.

At the time that we were living at Moor Top Mineral House was the home of Mr Grace the Mining Engineer for the Company, and consequently a man of some importance.

My friend William Stobart and I used to know Clifford, the son, who was about our own age, but I cannot remember much about the family. Perhaps I thought that they belonged to a different social class from us.

I was always a bit baffled by the appearance of the house, because I couldn't really tell whether it was one house which had had several additions to it, or whether the other buildings had originally been coach- houses and so on. They all seemed to be joined together, as indeed they are today, but each one having a different occupant.

I was aware that part of the house had been in use as a private school at various times over a long period, most recently occupied by Miss Hirst. It may be that, when I was quite young, the fact that the premises were used as a private school was sufficient to cause me to look upon this group of buildings with a kind of inquisitive respect.

I don't recall seeing much activity there by the time I was into my 'teens, so perhaps the school had ceased to exist as such, and became instead several separate homes. I remember the Poole family lived in one of the houses and another family named Sinclair, whose daughter Angela required daily attention and exercise, consequent upon her having had an accident, I believe.

At the other side of Abb Scott Lane was the home of Mr & Mrs Myers - Moorside House - quite a large group of buildings. This is where Mrs Myers went to live upon her marriage, and where she lived for the rest of her life.

This property was not erected by the Low Moor Company but by a distant relative of Mrs Myers' husband.

At the junction of Common Road and Abb Scott Lane was the corporation's dross staith, which I remember very well as being a place where we used to play, running and jumping around the mounds of dross and other road repairing materials such as ash, slag and broken stone. The staith was separated from the housing below by a short snicket; I used this snicket recently (1995) but the staith itself has disappeared, to be replaced by a modern house.

The first house below the staith was occupied by Dan Hellewell and his family. I don't think I ever knew what his job was, but I'm inclined to the view that he had an important position with the Victoria Mills Co., and so was possibly closely associated with Alfred Briggs.

The next house below Dan Hellewell's was the home of my piano teacher, Annie Mortimer and her parents. I'm not quite sure of the name of Dan Hellewell's daughter, possibly she was called Annie; I used to see her occasionally, especially when I went for my piano lesson; she would often be leaving after having had her lesson, just as I arrived for mine.

Some years later Annie Mortimer married Harry Clayton, and they lived in the large house in School Street which I believe was built by the Victoria Mills Company. Harry had an important job with the company, possibly as Company Secretary, but I'm not sure about this.

In Common Road, almost opposite the dross staith, was the very distinctive residence of West House, with West Cottage adjoining. This large block, standing in its own grounds was not actually built for the Victoria Mills Company, but built by the builder of the mills for his own occupation, later acquired by Alfred Briggs - mill owner and local benefactor.

It was he who left a number of bequests for the benefit of local people, originally intended for former employees, I believe. The Almshouses in Abb Scott Lane were erected and are maintained by the Trustees of the Alfred Briggs Trust, and an annual distribution of a sum of money from the Trust is also made to deserving cases.

I recall that many years ago there was a tennis court between West Cottage and Moorside Street, and as young lads will, we used to climb on to the top of the wall (and there was quite a large drop on the other side), we used to sit there watching the play, whilst one of the less disciplined among us used to call out rude remarks such as I never allowed past my lips, wherever I was. What a well-behaved boy I must have been, but then, all the boys hadn't been so fortunate in their choice of parents.

At the end of the drive at West House, and beyond the tennis courts, there were some coach houses or garages, above which were built two cottages. These cottages were in Moorside Street and they were the only dwellings on the street.

One of these cottages was occupied by a Mr Hammond and his family. I don't remember who the occupants of the other house were, even supposing that the house was occupied.

I don't remember a lot about the Hammond family, except to say that I remember that they had two daughters. They were a Catholic family, and I only mention this fact because there were so few in the area.

Mr Hammond was, I believe, Mr Briggs's coachman and perhaps later, his chauffeur/gardener, but it is a long time ago, and I've almost forgotten what his occupation was.

THIRTEEN

MOOR TOP - A WONDERFUL PLACE TO LIVE

Moor Top, where I really grew up, where I spent so many happy hours and where there were so many opportunities for natural youth activities, cries out for a few words of appreciation and a few recollections of some of the people who lived on Moor Top Road and thereabouts in the early twenties.

To begin with, much of this road is very old, as are the low cottages especially, of which there are a number, and which have been renovated and improved over the years. Many of these cottages, if not built by the Low Moor Company, were built during the early days of the Company's existence, i.e. about 1800 or even a little before that date.

During the years that I was growing up, there was always a rather dilapidated farm at the top of our street and in the middle of Moor Top Road. It seemed to be used, on and off, for all kinds of farm activities, but in the main I think it was used for stabling, or for keeping a few pigs and for storing a few loads of hay in the broken-down barn.

Behind the farm, and covering much of the area between the lower cemetery wall and the backs of the cottages, was a field in which we used to spend many happy hours. In the middle of this field was a large tree which we always called THE PLANE TREE, probably because that is what it was. I'm pretty certain the tree is still standing there today.

I shall never forget some of the characters of Moor Top, nor shall I forget some of the houses in which they lived. One or two of the houses were on the back and faced towards the field. The house in which Bob Plews and his son Ernest lived was such a dwelling.

From Abb Scott Lane, the first house on Moor Top Road stood out somewhat from the next couple of houses and perhaps this was so designed because behind it was the house that Bob Plews occupied. Jack Barraclough (who I always looked upon as being an old man) lived in this house with Leslie Kellett, who I believe was his grandson; Leslie always told us that his father lived in America, and by way of proof, he once produced a new football of a rather unusual (non-lacing) type, which he said his father had sent him from America.

I don't think Leslie enjoyed any of the advantages of being brought up by loving parents in a good home. Although he was one of the lads when playing games about the streets and in the fields, there were many times when he looked less than cared-for.

No doubt things started to improve for Leslie when he left school and started to work as an errand-boy and general assistant for Grays, Grocers at Bankfoot.

Everyone passing up or down Manchester Road in the Bankfoot area knew Leslie, with his bright red, beaming face and his cheerful whistle. He used to whistle at every one of the trams as they passed up or down the road, and the drivers, without exception, would respond to his whistle with a good stamp on the warning bell. It was like 'bedlam' sometimes but a healthy, cheerful 'bedlam'.

The next house along Moor Top Road was that of Tommy Slicer and his wife and family of two girls and one boy. I believe the girls were named Mary and Elsie, and the boy's name was Norman. They were all a few years older than I. I remember Mrs Slicer being very ill, and in fact she died when I was not very old, perhaps eight years of age.

Next to the Slicer's was, I think the home of the Ormondroyd's with their two boys - George and Fred - I don't remember if they had a sister. Fred was the younger of the two and I remember that he played cricket as a slow left arm bowler with Low Moor Cricket Club up at the Royds Hall ground.

I don't remember much about Fred after those days, but I used to see George frequently, when he lived in Netherlands Avenue, Odsal.

The Smalley family lived at this end of Moor Top Road too, possibly in the house next to Slicer's, or it might have been in the same house at a later date, after the Slicers moved away.

Next there was a house which had a kitchen and entrance built out in front of the line of most of the other houses. This was the home of Mr & Mrs Bartle and their four children - Herbert, the eldest, then James, Thomas and their sister Annie. Annie was a friend of my sister Evelyn, and about the same age; she used to come to tea sometimes, I recall.

If I remember correctly, there was a passage next to the Bartle house, and round the back was the entrance to the home of Mr & Mrs Crossland and their boys - Rowland, the eldest, Tom, the next and then Arthur the youngest. With the passing of the years I have lost sight of the older lads, but after he was married, Arthur lived in Shaw Street, as he still does, now as a widower, unfortunately.

I believe the next house after the passage was at one time occupied by Miss (or the Misses) Clayton, whose family had owned the builder's yard opposite their home. There was also a family called Smith who lived hereabouts, perhaps in the same house at a later date.

Mr Smith was a widower, and I remember his marrying again. He had two boys, both of them older than I. Irvine was the elder of the two, but more often called 'Ginger', for some reason. His younger brother's name was Bill. I lost sight of both these lads with the passing of the years.

The next houses on the top side of Moor Top Road were all joined up to the farm buildings. I think the first house was that of Mr & Mrs Harold Clark, who I believe had one daughter. Next to them was Mrs Wilks (Emma Jane I think she was called); she and her daughter Florence kept a little sweet shop in the house, the sweets being displayed on a table in front of the window.

Mrs Wilks was, according to my standards, a huge woman. There seemed to be a lot of very stout ladies on Moor Top Road, but Mrs Wilks was by far the largest. She never seemed to move more than a couple of steps from her 'cratch', and only then to serve her young customers. I used to visit her little shop frequently, but I never used to hang about after being served with my bar of chocolate or bag of sweets, because, to put it as kindly as I can, I found the atmosphere somewhat 'heavy'.

Next to Mrs Wilks and in the corner was the home of the O'Brien's - father, mother and I think four children, James, Elizabeth Ann, Emma and Mary. They seemed to be a very poor family, with 'little to go on' as we used to say; it was without any doubt a daily struggle to 'make ends meet'.

The farm buildings themselves came next, and beyond them was an open space which led to the back of the next lot of cottages and also gave access to the fields behind; before reaching the fields, however, there was, at the rear of the cottages, room for a small hen run and one or two rabbit hutches.

The first cottage past this opening was occupied by a man whom we will call 'Johnson', though that was not his name. He lived there with his wife and baby and I knew his name well enough.

'Johnson', as all the lads knew very well, was likely to arrive home on a Saturday afternoon much the worse for drink, and likely, too, to make quite a noisy spectacle of himself by trying to terrorize the entire neighbourhood with his challenging drunken antics.

We lads used to run out of his way, hiding behind walls, in order to observe the pantomime. We weren't really afraid of him, because we knew that we could move a lot quicker than he could, but we found it all very exciting, nevertheless. Our parents, on the contrary, were concerned for the safety of his own wife and child. I shall probably always remember those exciting times when the wild, belligerent, blond 'Johnson' arrived home on a Saturday afternoon.

Happily, such scenes are a thing of the past in this part of the world, and a good thing too.

I am unable to say who occupied the next two or three cottages along the road. There was the Barraclough family, and whilst I cannot remember the names of their parents, I do remember Jossie, Arthur, Sarah, and I think Mrs Crossland was another daughter older than Sarah.

Next to the end lived Norman Tordoff's Uncle Johnnie, I think that was his name. He was very popular with most of the lads of the village. He was the one who took it upon himself the duty of lighting the bonfire each year for our 'plot' celebrations, which we held on the open space almost facing his cottage at the end of Moor Top Road. This open space was, not surprisingly, used for housing, a few years later.

I remember that the bonfire was usually in the process of being lighted, just as we arrived home from school, consequently it was a frantic rush to get our teas eaten before dashing off to the bonfire. The last house of all along Moor Top Road and next to the Cemetery was the one occupied by Mortimer Laycock, his wife and children - Mary and Dan, both of whom were a few years older than I.

I have memories which never fade, of Mortimer going for his daily quart of beer from Henry Barraclough's shop at the top of Shaw Street. If I happened to enter the shop when Mortimer was being served, I always found the experience an interesting one, especially if Henry needed to tap a fresh barrel in order to serve him.

75

It was there, I suppose, that I learned to recognise the smell of beer as it was being drawn from the barrel. I must say though, that Mortimer always carried his jug slowly back home, where he drank his beer quietly, in his own house, disturbing nobody.

Just beyond the Laycock home was the entrance to the cemetery, opposite which were the gates of Harold Park.

As well as having our bonfire on that piece of ground, we also used to play cricket there in summer; the wickets being chalked on the cemetery wall. How we coped with the edge of the kerb, which ran almost exactly where we had to have our crease, I don't know - but we did.

Speaking of games, and outdoor games in particular, our repertoire grew as we did. When we were very young, simple games claimed our interest, but when we were older and stronger, we greatly enjoyed playing more vigorous games in which we expended a lot of energy.

Until the approach of Spring we had, to a large extent, been restricted to indoor games; when we were old enough we could hardly wait for the arrival of 'Pancake Tuesday', which heralded the season of outdoor activities.

The game of 'Whip and Top' was adequately catered for by the corner shops, well in advance of the PROPER time - 'Pancake Tuesday', but most parents knew in which drawer or cupboard last year's toys had lain hidden for so long.

One sees very few whips and tops about in these days, so it may be helpful to give a short description of these playthings. The whip was a light, round stick of twelve to fourteen inches in length and it had a small hole bored in it at one end; through this hole was threaded the 'lash', which was similar to a thin leather bootlace.

There were two kinds of top that I remember. One, the most expensive kind was a dumpy sort of top in plain or varnished wood, boxwood I believe. I never possessed one of those. The other kind of top, a much cheaper type, as well as being cheaper was also slimmer and taller. This model was usually dyed purple, red or green. Each one had a metal point or cone at its base to enable it to spin rapidly.

The technique for starting the top spinning is rather difficult to describe, but first one had to wind the 'lash' a couple of times around a groove just below the top's upper surface. The whip was jerked away from the top at the same time as the top was released. After some considerable practice it became possible, not only to make the top spin, but to keep it spinning for a minute or two, by continuing to lash it with the whip.

It was an acquired skill, of course, and some children were always better at it than others. It was, however, a harmless pastime which we much enjoyed for a time and until we moved on to some other game that took our fancy.

One such pastime which came out of hiding at about the same time of the year, was that of running with a hoop, sometimes called a 'bowl', which in local dialect sounded more like 'bahl'.

Girls used to run with a wooden hoop, which they used to beat with a wooden stick, but no boy would be seen running along the streets with such a feminine piece of equipment.

Boys had IRON hoops, which they propelled with a long handled iron hook. IRON hoops were for boys, and the local blacksmiths (of whom there were, in those days, several around Low Moor) would make an iron hoop with a hook to drive it and besides being more masculine, it could take a lot more ill-treatment than a wooden hoop, and would last for years - BUT WHERE DID THEY ALL GO?

Some parents, I recall, insisted that the blacksmith should supply the hook closed, or locked on to the iron hoop; this subtle device was considered to be much safer than having a hook that was detached.

The reason for this strategy was because hoops had been known to escape from the control of boys who were running with them, and if that should occur, there was always the danger of an accident, especially on a hill. In spite of this possibility, most boys, and I was one of them, preferred to have the hook free from the hoop.

We used to run miles, driving our hoops along, imagining ourselves to be all kinds of different characters such as charioteers, racing motorists and so on. We used to arrive back at home bathed in sweat from our efforts, but with our faces glowing with health and more than ready for a good wash (so mother said), followed by an equally good tea or supper.

The game of marbles (generally called 'taws' locally), was always eagerly awaited after the long, dark days of Winter and, like the whips and tops of the younger children, appeared on the streets as if obeying some law of nature.

I wasn't very good at marbles, but some lads possessed a large bag of 'taws', often passed on from elder brothers, or more likely that they had won from me; I, who had neither a brother nor very much skill, never seemed to have more than a pocketful, and that used to dwindle to nothing in the course of a couple of days.

I eventually came to the conclusion that I was not sufficiently assertive, as everyone else seemed to observe his own set of rules, the consequence of that being that it wasn't always easy to have a quiet, friendly game of 'taws'.

I don't think that marbles were as easily obtainable in my young days as they became later. Many of those that we used were glass 'alleys' from 'pop' bottles, where they had acted as stoppers when the bottles were filled.

I believe that 'pop' bottles were originally so called because when the stopper was forced down into the neck of the bottle, by the striking of a wooden implement which had been placed over the end of the bottle as a prelude to opening it, the result was a sharp 'POP' as the airtight seal was broken.

One version of the game involved placing an agreed number of marbles from each player, in a circle drawn in the dirt of the street and then in turn, aiming a 'pot knur' at them to try to remove a few from the circle. We used to roll a knur, sometimes rather vigorously, at the ring of marbles, and any that were knocked out of the ring were our winnings.

Some of the lads used what was known as an 'Iron Dobby', which was an iron ball-bearing, about an inch in diameter, and which was capable of wreaking havoc when clearing clay 'taws' from the ring. I never possessed one of these monsters myself, hence my lack of success at the game of marbles.

Just for the records, there was another version of the game which was intended to make the game simple. The first player used to roll his marble (a large pot knur) a short distance, say four or five feet along the ground, his opponent would then try to score a hit on the other's pot knur. The reward for being successful was one marble. There was a modification to the game, which somebody thought up, and this involved scoring with a 'span'.

I can't remember much about this rule except that we used to make quite a performance of kneeling down in the dirt and measuring with a hand span to check if a 'near miss' was within a span (the distance between little finger and thumb, at full stretch). This play went on, attacking and being attacked alternatively until the players grew tired of the game.

I was fond of cricket and football, and until I was in my late 'teens, when I began to play tennis, no other game could match them in my opinion.

There was another game of which I was very fond in my younger days, a game which seemed to have an affinity with the game of cricket - that was the game we called 'CATTY'. I sometimes heard the game being called 'PIGGY' in other parts of Bradford.

This game was played by the striking of a small piece of wood, such as a piece from a broken brush handle, about six inches long, with each of its ends sharpened to a point. the striking stick could be a part of the remainder of the brush handle, about thirty inches in length.

The small piece of wood - the 'CATTY' - was placed in the centre of a circle drawn on the ground, and the striker would tap one end of the pointed 'Catty', causing it to rise up into the air, to be hit smartly (in theory), by the striker, as far as possible.

This game, like most boys' games, was capable of many modifications, even sometimes in mid-game, which could lead to a certain amount of friction between the players.

The version I remember best was the one when the opponents took turns to see who could hit the 'catty' the greatest distance. It then became the task of the loser, who then became the 'MUGGER, to go and pick up the 'catty' and attempt, from that position , to throw it into the circle. His opponent had the choice of either taking a swipe at the catty, while it was still in the air, or wait until it landed on the ground, hopefully outside the circle, as it usually did.

He would then be free to repeat his original action, striking the catty again as far as possible, for his opponent to 'MUG IT' and throw it, once again in the direction of the circle. This could go on until either the 'mugger' threw the catty into the circle, or gave it up from sheer exhaustion.

I ought not to leave the subject of outdoor games without mentioning 'skipping'. This was really a girl's game, but sometimes on a summer evening it became a 'free-for-all'. Certainly, I remember that it did in Shaw Street, when half-a-dozen adults, parents and older children, used to get a lot of amusement from joining in a game of skipping, with a clothes line stretched halfway across the street. Happy Days. Gone for ever I'm afraid.

79

FOURTEEN

SERENDIPITY

The word 'SERENDIPITY' is one which seems to have crept up on me, unawares, which is to say that it was never in my vocabulary until a few years ago, and even then I was not all that sure of its meaning. However my reference book, 'OXFORD ENGLISH' gives the following definition of the word - 'THE MAKING OF PLEASANT DISCOVERIES BY ACCIDENT'. This clearly is a gift without which no writer can hope to succeed!

I had reached a point in these memoirs when I was asking myself "where do I go now ?". Glancing through an old Wesley Place Bazaar Programme dated 1911, I came across a small advertisement for 'HAYCOCK'S WONDERFUL OINTMENT' and after a moment or two I realised that this was 'SERENDIPITY' at work.

Dick Haycock was a figure who was easily recognisable as he walked the streets of Low Moor, for he was very dependent on his walking stick. He was rather badly disabled because of his lame leg. I knew him well because his name was often mentioned in our home and in that of my grandparents. It was no doubt as a result of hearing these adult conversations that I came to learn about Dick.

He, his wife Anne and their daughter Hilda, lived in School Street at number 47, by the entry into Tordoff Square. Next to them lived Anne Haycock's sister Maria Fox, unless in fact she lived in the same house, with the Haycocks, I'm not sure.

I have to confess that I knew nothing of Dick's involvement in the ointment business and I'm surprised that I never remember seeing any boxes of this wonderful ointment on sale at chapel bazaars and sales of work. I think it is more likely that by the time I was taking notice of things, he had ceased trading in the ointment due to lack of business.

One thing I had learned from listening to my parents' and grandparents' conversation was the fact that Dick was employed at the Low Moor Gas Works, down Cleckheaton Road.

This fact caused all Dick's friends some concern at the time of the Low Moor Explosion in 1916. Although I was not yet six years of age, somehow I realised that he might have been amongst those killed or injured; happily this was not the case. Once again, this reaction of mine might have been as a result of listening to my parents' conversation on the subject.

No doubt it was because of their connection with chapel that I came to know the members of the Haycock family so well, though I cannot recall that Dick was an active supporter.

Both Mrs Haycock and her sister were members of a strong Ladies' Meeting (The Devotional Hour), and Hilda Laycock, who later became Mrs Charles Ramsden, took part in sketches, partnered by Lily Kellett, quite often. These sketches which were performed by the young ladies were, I think, written and directed by Evelyn Taylor's Aunt Emily (Bateman). Hilda Ramsden, I recall, invariably played the role of a refined or rather 'posh' character.

Opposite the home of the Haycock family lived Stephen Hodgson, (always called 'Steam'!), his wife Sophia and the children Fred and Ada. 'Steam' sang in the chapel choir regularly, Fred only on special occasions, I think.

I remember 'Steam' particularly because, when I was no more than five years old, he was the one who sat next to the organ stool on the bass side. He was responsible for putting up the number of the next hymn, after each hymn had been sung as we only had the one central hymn board above the organ and this could only accommodate one hymn number at a time.

As I sat in the choir on the tenor side, next to the organ stool, and being young and inquisitive, I had lots of time for looking around and some of the things which are now remembered by few people, I found very interesting in those early days.

Although I didn't realise it at the time, the upper room possessed one of the earlier attempts to improve audibility in that very lofty building. At each side there were wires stretched across the hall from one end to the other, the intention being to enable the sound to carry better. I have no recollection that the system made the slightest difference to the congregation's ability to hear the preacher!

Another thing that claimed my interest was the chapel clock. This was a free-standing clock and a huge structure; the case looked as if it was made of pitch-pine - like the pews, and it stood on the top of the entrance vestibule which projected into the chapel at the back. In order to reach the clock, to wind up the mechanism, one had to climb a type of step-ladder attached to the back wall of the church, and which was concealed in a long narrow cupboard. I used to watch my father climbing this ladder to wind up the clock, and I couldn't wait until I was old enough to try it for myself.

A third matter of considerable interest to a small boy, was the hole in the floor. This was about thirty inches square, along one of the aisles. This aperture had, obviously, a wooden cover, and the purpose of this interesting hole was to enable extra seating and other items from the schoolroom below, to be pushed up through the hole when required for use in the chapel, and passed down again after use.

The narrow stone staircase which wound up from the schoolroom was hardly suitable for such traffic, and to use the front entrance of the chapel, apart from the fact that it was a long way round, had a number of steep steps, (there must have been at least eight or nine). So that excursion was out of the question. The hole, therefore, was a very good idea, that was much appreciated by succeeding generations.

I was always intrigued by two small boxes which were let into the vestibule wall at the back of the chapel. Each of these boxes had its tiny keyhole and its slot for the insertion of coins or banknotes (?) Across the face of each box was written in yellow letters - 'FREEWILL OFFERINGS'. I may be mistaken but it's my opinion that no-one had taken the trouble to open either of the boxes for years!

Before I leave the subject of the chapel and its activities, I ought to mention the fact that two of our ministers in those days (around the early 1920's) were the Rev Sam Davies and the Rev Arthur Bilsborough whose names are still remembered by a few of the former worshippers at School Street. They are remembered with affection as two of the finest and most friendly, devoted ministers we ever had.

Now I resume my reminiscences of people who attended School Street Chapel, and who in so many cases, lived nearby.

Further down School Street lived Charity Smith (Firth) and her husband, whose name I think was Willie, and their daughter Gertrude. Gertrude married Bernard Shaw and they lived in Mr and Mrs Smith's former home in School Street, I believe.

Near the top of School Street, and next to the little sweet shop that was opposite the chapel, lived Joe Henry Fox, his wife and children -Harry and Agnes. Sadly Mrs Fox died while the children were still quite young and Agnes had to assume the role of house-mother, which she did with great credit. She later married Dan Barraclough who had been living next door!

At the other side of the sweet shop lived John Woodhead and his wife Clara and next again lived Ellen Barraclough who was the caretaker of the chapel when I was small boy. I think her husband's name was Abram, and if so, he along with Isaac Knowles, was probably an executor for my grandfather's will.

Isaac Knowles lived with his family at the Union Road end of Fountain Street. He was a well-known figure at the chapel and I believe he was a Sunday School Superintendent, but that was before I started as a scholar there. He worked at 't'reight's shop' at the same time as my grandfather. I know this because I have a photograph of them both in a group of blacksmiths and wheelwrights, all shown in their working clothes.

Isaac Knowles' son Willie, and his wife, Sarah Lizzie, lived in the cottages (and I think there were two joined together) in Union Road, at the corner of School Street, where my great-aunt Martha lived, around 1920/21.

Before leaving the area of School Street I should mention that at the junction of North Street and School Street there had been some years ago, a shop with adjoining living accommodation. In 1904 this building was converted to a Cottage Baths, which was quite an innovation for Low Moor at that time and one can imagine how quickly it became a valuable amenity in the district, especially for the men who were employed on dirty jobs at the Ironworks and in the local pits. No doubt the baths would be extremely busy at the week-end!

I must say, though, that I cannot remember whether, in fact, it was ever in use during the time that we lived in Fountain Street, which would be between 1910 and 1914, though I assume that it would be in use then, and for some time afterwards.

I knew the building as 'The Baths', long after it had ceased to supply this service, and had been turned back into living accommodation again. Finally it disappeared altogether in the Low Moor Re-Building Scheme.

FIFTEEN

THE PICTURES

If I had informed any of my friends that I was going to the cinema on a Saturday afternoon, they would hardly have guessed that it was my intention to visit the Low Moor Picture House in Huddersfield Road. To us it was always ' t'pictures', the cinemas were in Bradford.

Neither Evelyn nor I were brought up to be regular visitors to the 'pictures', though I do remember the one occasion when I was taken by my grandmother to the cinema in Bradford - St George's Hall. This was during the First World War and my grandma had a great concern for the lads who were 'at the front' and who were shown on the screen. Although she rarely went to the pictures, this visit was a show of patriotism which perhaps made her feel a little better about the whole business of the war and her part in it.

Just occasionally, when the family had been out for a walk and a picnic over Royds Hall, through Judy Woods and on to Norwood Green, returning via Huddersfield Road, perhaps as a special treat Dad would take us to the evening performance at the pictures - a special treat indeed. This only occurred at holiday times such as Easter, Whitsuntide or during Carr Lane Tide week, which was always held at the same time as Bowling Tide, and Bradford Holiday Week.

As I grew older, along with some of my pals, I used to visit the Saturday afternoon 'RUSH' more frequently, and at other times during holidays when an extra performance would be put on for youngsters. I don't know if others had advance knowledge of these extra performances, but we used to have to take our chance, and sometimes we were disappointed, I remember.

The Picture House used to be managed by Mr Lush Senior and Austin. Austin's wife used to help, either in the booking office, or by checking tickets. Also I remember that Jim Throp used to be on duty as a kind of commissionaire, wearing his official hat, which looked like a second-hand tram-driver's hat. Perhaps this uniform was a legal requirement.

His daughter, Victoria was also employed at the Picture House as an usherette, showing the patrons to their seats, but this function was not allowed to operate very successfully at the Saturday afternoon 'RUSH'. Although I may be mistaken, I believe I remember Jim Throp's wife helping out as well. The Throp family, as I recall, lived in Thomas Street, just two or three doors from School Street.

To the youngsters of Low Moor, the exciting films were real attractions in those days, and the noise on Saturday afternoons was tremendous, especially when the film ended with either the hero or the heroine being left in an apparently hopeless position - tied to the rails in front of a fast-approaching train, or with hands and feet bound, hanging above a fiery pit or a whirlpool of boiling oil. As the film ended, across the screen flashed the words -

"TO BE CONTINUED NEXT WEEK"

We had to wait until the following week to see the result of all the trials and tribulations, and there was more than a possibility that we might not be able to be present at the next performance. Oh misery.

The frantic cheering and the ear-splitting shouts of encouragement almost (but not quite) rivalled the noise that burst forth when the film mechanism broke down and the picture disappeared from the screen. Oh dear. What a catastrophe, and to be greeted with such shouts of derision.

We, along with the management of course, were accustomed to these interruptions and we realized that the film would be repaired, and the story resumed, in a matter of minutes, to a deafening roar of approval from the juvenile audience.

In spite of the fact that we were all very young, or perhaps because of it, we enjoyed to the full the performances of Mary Pickford, Douglas Fairbanks, Charlie Chaplin, Buster Keaton, Harold Lloyd and our very first favourite - Pearl White, along with all the other stars of yesteryear.

Which thoughts lead me to think about 'COMICS'. When I began to have a weekly comic delivered to my home, I was beginning to feel quite grown-up. Well, my grandma had 'THE CHRISTIAN HERALD' and 'THE SUNDAY COMPANION' delivered weekly, and my mother had 'HOME CHAT' delivered, so I wanted to be like them. My choice was 'FILM FUN', and I enjoyed the antics of the comics that we saw on the screen.

Later, I remember that both William and I moved on to the more grown-up comics and while William went for the 'ROVER', my choice was 'ADVENTURE'. Of course there was a lot of 'swapping' of comics, so we read all the comics that we could get hold of, as we moved towards adulthood.

SMOKING, by men, was taken for granted in those days. Few people seemed to be aware of the dangers of smoking. My grandfather smoked a pipe all his adult life, and so did my father. Neither of them, in common with most of their companions, had the slightest awareness of the life-threatening effects of tobacco.

There were those, of course, who called smoking a dirty, evil-smelling habit, but no more than that. It was a fact of life that most men smoked. Many of them smoked cigarettes - Will's 'WOODBINES', 'CAPSTAN FULL STRENGTH' and Players' 'NAVY CUT'.

For boys such as myself, one of the benefits accruing from men's smoking of cigarettes, lay in the fact that most packets of cigarettes (but not the 2d packets of 'Woodbines') contained Cigarette Cards.

From the point of view of publicity only, Cigarette Cards were a most acceptable idea with the general public, but with schoolboys they were popular in the extreme. Most of the different series were colourful, well printed and often educational too.

There were interesting series on many different subjects such as animals, birds, motor cars, cricketers, footballers etc., and most boys loved to collect 'CIG CARDS'.

It was quite a normal activity for a boy to approach an absolute stranger on the street, to enquire "ave you any Cig Cards, Mister?' Sometimes the boy might even add 'Please'. In this way we were able to amass quite a collection of cards, and we played several different games with our friends, in order to win (or lose) more.

The game I liked best was called 'Skimmers', and this involved standing one card up against a wall, and from a distance of three or four feet we used to throw or 'Skimmer' a card from between our index and middle fingers towards the card, with the intention of knocking the card over. If you were successful, then all the cards that lay on the ground at that moment became yours - you had won them.

Baines's Famous Football Cards were very popular with some groups of lads, but for some reason I was never closely involved with them and they never seemed to claim my interest in the same way that cigarette cards did.

I have some recollection of Baines's Football Cards being available at most sweet shops. They were sold in what we called 'Lucky Bags', but what was in the bags in addition to the two or three shield-shaped paper emblems bearing the name of some football club, I cannot now recall.

Of course, any game thought up by we lads was just one more way of re-distributing the cards amongst one's mates (by winning or losing them). It was never my good fortune to build up a large stock of these cards, as some lads did, and perhaps this is the real reason why my recollection of the games that we played is more than a little hazy.

I was recently looking through the Blotter and Year Book issued by the Low Moor Primitive Methodist Chapel to mark the Re-opening in 1924 after extensive alterations.

These alterations had involved the installation of electric lighting, structural alterations to the rooms previously known as the 'Cottage', in order to make one large and extremely useful room out of two small and inconvenient rooms. All this was followed by complete re-decoration.

Among a number of interesting items which I came across in the Blotter, was a list of Chapel officials, with their addresses. Alonzo Adams (generally called 'Lonza), one of the Chapel Stewards, was shown as living at number 8, Tyrrel Street, an address which I knew as well as my own. My grandfather, who had died in 1921, had lived at this address and it was a pleasant surprise for me to learn that Alonzo Adams had moved into the house that my grandfather had occupied before he died.

The Adams family were very active at the chapel. Edwin, Alonzo's brother, was one of the Society Stewards, along with John Kellett. It was Edwin Adams, I remember, who first asked me to consider taking a 'Note to Preach', in other words, to begin the process of training to become a Local Preacher, which I eventually did.

Edith Adams was closely involved with Chapel and Sunday School activities, particularly in relation to the Women's Devotional Hour.

It was only recently, (March 1995) that I learned of the death of Edith Adams' daughter, Doris, a few months earlier. I remembered that Doris had been a strong supporter of the Tennis Club's activities when it was in its infancy. I had many a game with her when I was just learning the game.

87

Doris gained something of a reputation as a contralto vocalist, and I well remember that, in the days when 'Messiah' was an annual event at the 'PRIMS', she sang the contralto solos one year, for which she received warm congratulations, I believe.

She was also a member of the RANTER REVELLERS' Concert Party, which was the conception of Mrs Willie Barraclough in the first place I believe, supported by Evelyn Taylor and John Swaine (Jack) Hardy.

Following the recent death of Bertha Priestley, apart from Doris Adams's husband, Sidney Jelfs, Evelyn Hardy is the only member of the 'Ranter Revellers' still living today (1995).

Mention of Sidney Jelfs reminds me that, as quite a young man, he came to live with his aunts, who kept a little confectioner's shop at the top of Cartwheel Street, (later re-named Cartwright Street to appease local sensitivities, one supposes.)

I think Sidney, who was not a Yorkshireman, came to live with his aunts in following the death of one of his parents, but I'm not sure about this. The sisters were called Naylor - M.H. and M. I don't think I ever knew what the initials stood for, but I daresay I could make what my mother used to call a 'foul', or a wild guess.

Sidney served his apprenticeship with George Booth, Joiner and Undertaker, and after his marriage to Doris they went to live in Liversedge, where I remember visiting them on one occasion when I was taking a service there for a former local preacher, well known in the district - Ex Corporal Briggs.

I don't remember the circumstances, but after Doris and Sidney left Liversedge I believe they actually moved back to where Sidney had come from, to take over a family business which he inherited. After this time I used to hear about them only very rarely.

I realize that there are quite a number of features associated with the streets of Low Moor that I have not yet referred to, so I will endeavour to put this right.

When I have been visiting the Wesleyan Reform Chapel recently, I have wondered, as I have many times in the past, what purpose the black painted wooden hut was now serving, as it stands, and has stood for the past seventy years at least, at the junction of Manor Row and Union Road, just below the front entrance of the chapel.

I have known this hut for most of my life, looking, it seems to me, exactly as it did seventy or eighty years ago, and why it should, I simply cannot imagine. I know this, if the hut had been standing in my garden all this time, it would have fallen into disrepair and would have been replaced, perhaps twice in that period of time. Why it is still standing there I cannot imagine.

And why, when so many of Low Moor's mills, warehouses, shops and, above all, houses, have disappeared - I just wondered what special features kept this black wooden workshop still standing there.

Whether the hut is still actually in use, I do not know. I remember that many years ago it belonged to a James Sharp - Undertaker. By way of evidence, I have a black-edged envelope which contains a satin notice of the death of a Low Moor resident.

The printed notice on satin seems to have been a common practice by which friends and relatives were notified of a person's demise.

The envelope bears the name - James Sharp, Union Road, with no number, and I assume the address was of his workplace, but of course he may have lived in Union Road too.

My grandparents, who lived in Tyrrel Street during most of the years that I knew them, always kept a supply of Dry Ginger Ale at the top of the cellar steps. I am not aware that they consumed much of this fizzy beverage themselves, but I am inclined to the view that, as grandparents will, they kept a small stock of it just for me in the first place, my sister being much too young to appreciate such refreshment.

I remember that the suppliers of Mineral Waters were Levi Boocock & Son, whose works were in the little valley just off the Halifax Road at Shelf. I believe that their delivery cart used to be driven around the streets of Low Moor about once a fortnight, and granddad's order was invariably the same on each visit - two bottles of Dry Ginger Ale.

Of course the milkman was another regular visitor, more regular in fact, as he came to our door every day.

I can't be quite sure, but when we lived on Fountain Street, our milk was delivered by John Willie Platts, who lived in Park Road, although another milkman, Harker Shaw, lived almost exactly opposite us across the street. For some reason , when we moved to Moor Top, our milkman there became Joe Bairstow, who used to come all the way from Dean House Farm at Shelf.

It's my belief that all small boys were intrigued by the milkman's custom of ladling milk into the customer's jug from the can which he carried from door to door, and then providing that 'LITTLE DROP EXTRA'. That. it seemed to me, was a most important ritual that should NEVER be overlooked - and in my experience it never was.

Another very popular salesman along our streets was Freddie Wells. I distinctly remember (and how these trifles stay in the mind) that painted on the side of his cart was the name - CHAS. F. WELLS, but he was known to everyone, even to youngsters like me, as 'FREDDIE'.

Apart from the fact that he was a regular visitor along the streets of Low Moor, Moor Top and perhaps down 't'Low End' as well, I am sure that Freddie did quite a profitable trade selling green groceries from his cart at the stable in Common Road. I recall that Mrs Minnie Priestley's daughters used to get the family's vegetables from Freddie's Saturday morning stall, and so did many other families too.

SIXTEEN

WHITSUNTIDE WALKS

My father was a dedicated supporter of the Co-operative Stores in Low Moor, but as a convinced Liberal, I don't think he had any leanings towards the Co-Operative movement and its philosophies.

He thought that it was appropriate nevertheless, to concentrate his support on the local society, and so when it came to the Co-op Galas, he was proud to act as marshall for the Low Moor section of the procession, when the children from the various branches in Low Moor, Wibsey and Bankfoot, used to join up and march in procession to the site of the Gala, with a few parents and other adults as supervisors.

The Gala was held annually in the fields which were in the triangular area between Haycliffe Lane and St. Enoch's Road, part of which was occupied by the Great Horton Cricket Club's grounds, and where later, Grange Grammar School was located.

When I first began to take part in the procession, I remember that we had a small brass band, followed by a couple of decorated carts which carried some adverts for the Co-op's products. As time passed, however the band became smaller until eventually it ceased to appear at all and unless I am mistaken, even the decorated cart couldn't manage it any longer, as far as Low Moor.

I've almost forgotten what we did when we reached journey's end; I suppose we were all allocated an area according to the branch that we came from and then large milk cans containing hot, freshly-made tea were brought to us in the field. I suppose too, that we each took our own mugs (or our parents produced them at the appropriate time) after which we were issued with long currant buns.

I don't remember any 'afters', but I'm sure that the Co-op Bakery and Confectionery Department would come up with a sweet bun or a cake 'to finish off with', but I'm afraid that sometimes these extra treats didn't reach everyone.

Once we had all fed, then it was the time for the children's races , but although I probably took part, I seem unable to remember anything about them. Obviously they didn't make a LASTING impression upon ME.

What I do remember is that we used to enjoy playing 'roly-poly' down the embankment from St Enoch's Road, rolling down the grassy slopes, from top to bottom. That, we did enjoy.

I recall too, that word used to get around to the effect that the decorated carts were being dismantled, which meant that displays which had involved the use of provisions such as 'LUMP SUGAR',for example, became our targets and we raced off to get near the head of the queue in order to fill our pockets with Lump Sugar, and other pocketable items. This was all very exciting and I suppose that even though, at the end of the day I expect we were all tired out, we were also completely satisfied with all the different activities.

The various processions which had converged on the Co-op Gala fields early in the afternoon, had one object, of course, which was to get as many of the members' children to the site of the Gala as efficiently as possible.

It seemed to me though, at the time,that compared with our Sunday School's Whitsuntide 'Walk', the Co-op procession was a very dull affair indeed, but then, it was plain to everyone that the aims of the different organisations were also rather different.

Whilst the Co-op tried to give the children a good time, it was hard for them to disguise the fact that the whole exercise was something of a publicity stunt.

On the other hand, the Sunday Schools of the district were concerned not only to carry on old traditions, but also to demonstrate to the general public, (by publicity if you like) the sheer joy that was to be gained by way of Christian Service and by the proclamation of the Christian Gospel.

The Whitsuntide Walk was eagerly awaited by the children and by most of the local residents as well, (whether interested in the aims of the Churches or not), as a joyous, happy occasion.

As far as we at the 'PRIMS' were concerned, the excitement began quite early, around nine-thirty on the Tuesday morning. The forthcoming attractions had been discussed at some length by those who were on the Choir Trip, the previous day, for the Choir Trip was always held on Whit Monday.

I remember that coal carts used to appear outside the 'Cottage', in James Street. Sometimes there would be one and sometimes two, which had been carefully 'swilled down', to remove all traces of coal dust from them.

At one time, the first job for the men used to be the erection of the banner on one of the carts, which announced to all and sundry exactly who we were - though I seem to remember that our banner had got into such a state of disrepair that eventually it ceased to be produced at all, and stayed in its hiding place getting damper and smelling mustier, year by year.

The male teachers then used to carry the harmonium and stool from the schoolroom, lifting them on to the cart. After leaving enough space for the conductor, the remaining space was filled with small chairs from the Primary Department.

While this work was going on, the female teachers, armed with crêpe paper of many different hues, and with lots and lots of drawing pins, were busy decorating the cart or carts, and hoping fervently that there would be no sudden downpour to spoil all the arrangements.

Strangely enough, I cannot recall that there were many (if any) occasions when the procession had to be abandoned, or even curtailed because of rain.

While the decorating was being carried out, there was also plenty of activity in the schoolroom. All the copper tea urns and the large enamel jugs were washed out with boiling water, so as to be ready for the great feast.

Long tables were erected, and benches were arranged down each side of the table, because the older members used to have their teas on separate tables, properly served, with BUTTER on the cut-up buns.

All the crockery was produced and examined, Then, in the course of the morning, several trays of currant buns were brought in from the bakers, whoever they happened to be.

By twelve o'clock, things were beginning to become organised, but I remember that there was always a rush at home to have a meal , get washed and changed and be back at Sunday School for half-past-one.

While we were assembling, the hymn sheets were brought out; these were generally the ones that had been used at the Sunday School Anniversary the previous year, or even the same year when the Anniversary happened to fall on Whit Sunday.

In due course, everything was ready. The scholars were all gathered together in their age groups or classes, and the Primary children were found seats on the carts, along with one or two teachers, who we used to think were very lucky to be able to ride. Then, it was time for the procession to begin.

My father was often in charge of the music department. If he wasn't conducting the singing himself, (and he usually was) then he played the harmonium. I used to think that no-one could accompany the singing better than my Dad, and in fact, I think that he often thought so too.

He used to tell me sometimes, that when he learnt to play, he began first of all on a harmonium (or American Organ as they were often called), so he knew how to get the best out of the instrument. It was later that he switched to the piano, and later still that he began to have lessons on the pipe organ at the chapel.

As far as I can recall, in the early days we didn't join up in procession with other Sunday Schools, gradually the idea of a united 'WALK' began to be considered and we eventually joined up with the Wesleyan Reform Sunday School, with John Bartle conducting the singing and my father playing the organ.

We walked around the streets, stopping to sing a few hymns at pre-arranged points, as we had been doing for some years, but previously as separate Sunday Schools, each going its own way.

The idea of organising a United Whit Walk involving all the Sunday Schools in Low Moor, although at the back of the minds of a few dedicated Sunday School workers from time to time, was still a few years away from fulfilment. Desirable though the conception seemed to be to a few forward-looking people, we were not quite ready for such a bold measure.

SEVENTEEN

DYING CUSTOMS

Before I allow my enthusiasm to carry my thoughts away beyond the proper limits of these memoirs, which are meant to cover the years 1910 to 1926, I should now record a few of the incidents and occurrences which have not, so far, found a place in these pages. For instance, one or two things come to mind which are associated with my life on Fountain Street, and I think that the first of these, which I think is worthy of mention, is the mill 'whew', buzzer or hooter, which no-one could ignore.

I'm not very sure about the times when these different hooters were sounded to indicate starting times, both early morning and re-start after dinner-time break, when the engines were started up again.

We had no B.B.C. in those days, to give us Greenwich Mean Time, so even the mill master's timing wasn't always strictly accurate, with the result that we were likely to have, in various parts of the district, a succession of hooters sounding one after the other, some times a few minutes apart.

I have forgotten which hooters used to sound each day, with the exception of Victoria Mills, of course, because that was virtually at the end of our street. I also remember the one at Henry Birkby's brick works in Wilson Road, Wyke. This one I recall sounding every working day at dinner-time at either a quarter past or half-past one.

If I was up early when the 'whews' sounded, I would hear at the same time the 'clacking' sound of the clogs of the women and the girls as they hurried along the street past our window, their heads covered with grey or black woollen shawls. I suppose my mother wore clogs and shawl when she started work in the mill as a weaver. This was before I was born, but I can't recall the shawl she used to wear, but on the other hand, I remember quite distinctly the shawl that my grandmother wore.

It was a loosely knitted, wool shawl in an unusual kind of port wine shade. I've never forgotten it, it was so outstanding, because of its colour. She wore this shawl a great deal and for a number of years when visiting shops or calling upon friends, but definitely not for Chapel or other special occasions. At those times she wore a kind of long, black overcoat, or sometimes a short black jacket and skirt, with a large black hat, as was the fashion amongst womenfolk in those days.

Looking back, I have been a little surprised to discover that breakfast cereals are not quite the modern innovation that I tended to think. Of course porridge has been eaten for breakfast, and at other times, for centuries. I remember that my grandma had a lot of faith in 'GRAPE NUTS' and she used to ensure that I got a generous helping of her favourite cereal, whenever I was there for breakfast or supper.

My grandparents were very faithful readers of the 'CHRISTIAN HERALD', which I remember was delivered each week to their home in Tyrrel Street, but I don't remember any other weekly, such as 'HOME CHAT' for instance, being delivered.

I can't be sure about this, but I think they must have had an evening paper delivered, for where else would they get their toilet paper? I don't think that the 'CHRISTIAN HERALD' on its own would suffice, and in any case, I think that they used to pass this paper on to another, like-minded friend.

I remember the weekly ritual when my grandfather used to fold old papers in such a way that it became a simple matter to take a sharp knife - a carving knife usually - and slice the paper along the folds, to produce half-a-dozen sheets of the appropriate size from each page of newsprint, to be hung on a nail behind the door of the W.C.

When we lived in Fountain Street, the door to our house possessed a very large, box-like lock, which required a very large, iron key to lock and unlock it. It was just the same at Moor Top, with a large lock and a heavy key, but eventually my parents must have tired of carrying the heavy key around and decided to have a smaller lock fitted with a far lighter key.

This lock was the highly spoken-of YALE lock which required a much smaller and lighter key that was far less cumbersome in the pocket or handbag. At first this was something of a slight disadvantage. It proved to be too easy, when leaving the house, to drop the latch in order to lock the door, forgetting to take the key with you.

After this had occurred once or twice, before we got used to the new system, my parents discovered that there was some advantage in having a six- or seven-year old boy who was as brave as he was nimble, so, when they found themselves locked out, the simple solution proved to be to pop him through the grate, down into the coal-cellar, and then it was a case of going through the keeping cellar and up the steps to unlock the door. For a little while, this procedure had to be carried out frequently.

I cannot claim to have been an expert on the shops of Low Moor, but I wrote earlier about one or two of the shops that I visited fairly regularly, but there were a number of shops that I never ever had cause to enter.

In this category was the shop owned by Edwin Slicer in Huddersfield Road. The building was very well known because of the clock on the front, which was particularly noticeable because, instead of the usual numerals around the clock face, it had the owner's name in bold letters.

Edwin Slicer's advert in Wesley Place's Naval Bazaar programme held in 1911, states that he was a Watchmaker, Jeweller and General Dealer. Quite a tradesman apparently, but I think he must have ceased to trade before I grew up.

I also mentioned earlier that as well as Public Houses, Butchers Shops and Fish and Chip Shops, Low Moor also possessed, what seemed to me to be an abnormally large number of Boot and Shoe Makers for such a small community. I counted no fewer than seven such shops, which figure includes one tradesman who described himself as a Boot Maker and Clogger - and these were just the traders who advertised in the Wesley Place Chapel's 'Naval Bazaar' programme'.

A shop that was always a point of interest for me was that of Winterburn's, which used to have a set of swings on the land adjoining the shop, just below Harold Park gates, in Park Road. There for a copper or two. you could spend a little time swinging away to your heart's content.

With the passage of time, and with the changes that are always taking place in children's pastimes, the swings failed to be an attraction any longer, and eventually even the shop itself closed down.

When writing about the shops of Low Moor as they were in former days, one cannot overlook the Post Office opposite Victoria Square in Huddersfield Road. This small Post Office was a busy place and Mr Rowley, the Postmaster, and his wife ran a little shop along with the official Post Office duties.

They were very well respected in Low Moor. Mrs Rowley - Peggy -, coming from further north - she was a 'Geordie' I believe , but I've no doubt that she soon became used to our accents, as we did to hers, since we were all Northerners.

Some folks might be of the opinion that eighty years ago the streets of Low Moor were dull and uninteresting places, especially to the housewives who lived there. The same could be said about the streets of Bankfoot, Wibsey and Oakenshaw, but in fact nothing could be further from the truth.

The fact that houses generally had no indoor 'facilities', meant that whether from choice or design, women tended to spend more time out-of-doors, particularly in summertime, which gave plenty of opportunity for meeting neighbours who lived at the other end of the street. Time for a bit of gossip, time for exchanging information (in whispers, because of the children) about the latest local scandal. Oh yes, there was always 'plenty going on', on the streets of Low Moor!

Apart from the gossip, just one of the regular happenings was the visit to the street of the organ- grinder or barrel organ man, always referred to as the 'TINGALARY MAN', I don't know why. It always sounds to me as if it has an Irish origin, and what is more, I never really knew how to spell the name. Of course that wasn't important as we youngsters pestered our mothers for a coin to put in the organ grinder's tin, whether or not he had a monkey.

Thinking about organ-grinders reminds me of the fact that the 'KNIFE-GRINDER' used to come along the streets, wheeling his grindstone and treadle and calling 'KNIVES TO GRIND', 'SCISSORS TO GRIND'. If we had any work for him at all, it was usually the carving knife or the scissors that required an edge putting on them.

As my mind ranges over the years that are gone,(the labyrinthine years of my growing-up) there was one activity associated with Chapel and Sunday School that I suppose I shall remember for the rest of my life.

Christmas time was, as was to be expected, rather exciting, even in the years when we were approaching our 'teens. This was not because of Santa Claus, and the gifts, but because of Christmas Carolling. Because my father was the Choirmaster at the Chapel, Christmas was always a very musical season in our house.

Not only did we enjoy singing carols around the piano along with friends at home, but we used to go out from the Sunday School, setting off just before midnight on Christmas Eve, to sing for members and friends, especially those who were confined to their homes by reason of age or infirmity.

We lads used to enjoy this late night parading about - well, there were always GIRLS around, and you couldn't say that things weren't just a bit exciting at two and three o'clock in the morning, despite the fact that we had all been most carefully brought-up.

Before setting off, it was someone's job to see that a large pan of previously steeped and boiled peas was put on the gas ring in the kitchen, to simmer for two or three hours. When we returned from our carolling, they would usually just be ready for us to sit down to an early breakfast.

We used to visit many homes in the neighbourhood of the chapel and also visited people as far away as Wesley Place and Odsal Top. We always began by singing outside someone's door on the stoke of midnight, the first verse of 'CHRISTIANS AWAKE' to the accompaniment of Lister Stead's melodeon.

As we came to the end of the verse, someone would knock on the door to gain admittance, or the door would be opened by someone on the inside, waiting with bated breath (?) to receive us.

The leader of the group, often my Dad as Choirmaster, would wish the people being visited 'THE COMPLIMENTS OF THE SEASON'; there would then be a few moments for greetings all round, after which the hosts would be asked "What would you like us to sing next?"

If they had a piano, we would sometimes be asked to sing to a piano accompaniment, otherwise Lister Stead used to accompany the singing on his melodeon, if the carol was one in his repertoire.

As well as the carols which we sang to the usual well-known tunes, there were a number of carols which were sung to tunes that had been sung for many years, perhaps from 'Services of Song' from the past. There used to be a few yellowing copies of these old, traditional carols in drawers and cupboards in Sunday School, and there were also a few in the possession of one or two chapel folks like ourselves.

One of the most popular was 'O'ER THE GREEN HEDGE', and there were several arrangements for 'HARK, THE HERALD ANGELS SING' and 'IT CAME UPON THE MIDNIGHT CLEAR'.

These melodies, because of the rousing refrains which they had been given, had been kept alive from a time before many of us were born, though anything traditional is today, in the present climate, in grave danger of being lost for ever.

I recall the times when, after we had finished our carolling and had consumed our hot peas, it could have been getting on for four o'clock in the morning before we left the 'cottage', as the men used to enjoy sitting around the fire talking and smoking their pipes.

I remember too, when I was about nine or ten years old that it hardly seemed worthwhile going to bed, except that because my sister was so much younger , the visit of Santa Claus was still something to cause excitement. A further important ingredient of the Christmas Season was that I needed to be up early in order to go 'letting Christmas in'.

This was another old custom that was struggling to survive, by which young boys such as myself, used to go around to the houses of a few neighbours (those where we knew that we would be welcome), and shout through the keyhole or letter box - "WILL YOU LET CHRISTMAS IN?"

Usually we were gladly received and given a copper or two, (which was really the object of our visit anyway), and with our thanks we expressed our good wishes for "A MERRY CHRISTMAS AND A HAPPY NEW YEAR".

If the ritual of 'Letting Christmas in' was fast disappearing, even more so was this true of the traditional custom of 'MUMMING'. One or two members of the Stead family, namely Walter and Elsie (Coldwell), made heroic efforts to keep the custom alive. I think I was approaching my 'teens the last time I dressed up to go 'MUMMING'.

'MUMMING' I would have described as CAROL SINGING IN FANCY DRESS. Those taking part used to go around the neighbourhood on New Year's Eve, singing carols at a few selected houses. The really keen 'MUMMERS', such as Walter Stead, invariably appeared with soot-blackened faces, or wearing masks and fancy dress, such as grandma's nightgown.

Dressed as he was, I couldn't help thinking how like his mother Walter was, in spite of the sooty disguise. 'MUMMING' was however, a rapidly dying tradition and by the time I was into my 'teens', it was virtually lifeless.

I wrote earlier about the impressive Sunday School Anniversaries that we used to have at School Street 'PRIMS'. In order to be able to accommodate all the Sunday School children AND an augmented adult choir, a large platform was constructed from previously prepared wooden planks and supports that had been stored beneath the existing platform since the previous year's Anniversary.

This extension was erected by the men, in front of the choir stalls in time for the final rehearsal. Some of the men, such as Lister Stead, were joiners by trade, and very strong men some of them were too, so that erecting the platform was child's play to them.

I remember an incident that occurred one year at the final rehearsal. The organist was a former organist at our chapel, Willie Barraclough, organist at Wesley Place; my father was the conductor.

During a break in rehearsal, I remember my father stepping backwards from the music stand, and falling off the platform on to the floor, with a tremendous crash, for he was quite a big, heavily built man.

I raced round to him from my position in the choir stalls to help him up and on to the front pew. He was, for a moment or two, quite dazed, but to everyone's relief, after a short time he seemed little the worse and I suppose he thought ' THE SHOW MUST GO ON'.

I think he felt the bruising for several days afterwards, but the Anniversary Services went ahead without any further hitches that I was aware of.

There was an occasion that comes to mind when, after all the rehearsing that we had done, on the morning of the Anniversary, it began to look as if there was a distinct possibility that my dad would never get there. The reason for our doubts was a most unusual one, almost a once-in-a-lifetime happening.

The year was 1924, the year of the BRITISH EMPIRE EXHIBITION, which was held at Wembley. My Dad was a member of a party from the B.D.A. which went on an excursion to the exhibition. I cannot remember just what time they left Bradford for London, but I know that they were expected back at home early on Sunday morning - the morning of the Sunday School Anniversary. Imagine how we felt when nine o'clock arrived and no sign of father, who we knew would expect to be at his post no later than a quarter-to-ten.

I think it was about nine-thirty when he walked in, as composed and cheerful as if he had just been out to check on the weather. Few people down at the chapel knew anything of our anxiety that morning; there were no telephones then, to enable anxious wives to get in touch with the wives of other trippers, so as to share the worry. Of course, everything went ahead quite happily, as it always did.

EIGHTEEN

IMPRESSIONS OF SCHOOL DAYS

Those were the years when I was a scholar at Grange Road Secondary School, without achieving very much in the way of scholarship, and without making much of a mark of any kind, not even in sport though I enjoyed immensely playing both football and cricket. Years later, however, seeds which were planted at Grange, slowly began to germinate and make my life fuller and richer than had seemed possible in the earlier days. I was never taught Latin, but the phrase 'Nil desperandum' began to have meaning for me, - I had just been a slow learner.

The influence which some of the masters had upon me, as well as the subjects that they taught, proved to be life-enriching. It goes without saying therefore, that music under Meanwell Henton and Edmund Priestley was, for me, an enduring influence and one that has lasted until the present time.

I was an enthusiastic member of the school choir, which really came into its own at the school Speech Day held, in those days, in the Mechanics' Institute. We also gave a few concerts at various venues. I remember singing at one or two chapels and churches, and I can even remember one or two of the pieces from our repertoire, pieces that we used to sing, sometimes with real gusto.

It was never my joy to receive a prize at the SPEECH DAY presentations, but one thing I will always keep in my mind, and that was to see, year after year the large frame of the late Frank Musson walking down the aisle and ascending the platform to claim, not one but several prizes. Oh how I envied him.

This very human reaction to someone else's success didn't prevent me from giving of my very best as we raised our voices (while we still had them), in such contributions as 'The Turtle Dove' for instance. I also recall that we used to sing with particular fervour 'Sir Eglamore' and perhaps with less gusto and just a little passion, 'O Mistress Mine'.

I remember that I enjoyed singing both these ballads and several others, the names of the composers of which I cannot now recall, though I should.

The school orchestra used to perform nobly on the special occasions, delighting all of us with such items as 'Eine Kleine Nachsmusik'.

I remember Meanwell Henton as an extremely kind and helpful man who found it easy, I'm sure, to find scholars most willing to be helpful in return.

He used to conduct the school orchestra, and the choir was trained by Edmund Priestley. The accompanist for the choir rehearsals used to vary from time to time, but generally I think it was Mr Slinger who played for concerts.

I knew Mr Slinger best as a Maths teacher, of whom I was slightly in awe - Maths not being my best subject - whilst Mr Ogden, who was also my Maths teacher but at a different time, was in a similar mould to Mr Henton, a nice, quiet-spoken, friendly gentleman.

Maths and algebra were subjects that I never really understood during my first couple of years , and it was only later that they began to make any sense; naturally, I didn't show much improvement for a long time, as I'm sure my school reports would reveal. Fortunately I don't think my parents understood them either, so I got away without much censure on that score.

I considered French to be one of my stronger subjects, so I suppose I must have been just about average in the class. Mr Furlong was my French teacher for most of the time, though I do recall that we also had some lessons conducted by Miss Stead.

I was never very good at Art, but even so, I had the greatest respect for the Art master - Mr P.A.Antill. I think of him now as possessing many of the same qualities as Mr Henton and Mr Ogden - two of the nicest, quiet-spoken teachers it was my privilege to know in those days.

A draughtsman I certainly was not, nor am I today, but I still possess a copy of 'Heath's Practical French Grammar', which, in Mr Antill's Art class I re-bound, as an exercise in bookbinding.

Mr Antill showed us by his own work what was possible and I have not forgotten that on the wall of the Main Hall hung an example of that work - a framed copy of the poem 'If I should die' by Rupert Brooke, beautifully written in illuminated italic script.

I have often wondered what happened to this work of art after the school left Grange Road. I remembered the opening lines especially, during the war years when I was serving in the R.A.F., in the deserts of Iraq; it was there, in that foreign land, that the words had a particular significance for me.

The book - 'Heath's French Grammar', was given to me by Mr Greenwood the English master as a reward for a poem that I had contributed as my homework, following one of his lessons. I recall that I always looked upon Mr Greenwood as a kindly old gentleman, though he couldn't have been all that old, but, to me he always seemed to be so much older than any of the other masters, even older than one of the oldest - Mr Barraclough - who was sometimes in charge of us for the football period. I just found it impossible to imagine Mr Greenwood on the football field.

The one master who surely impressed everyone who passed through the school was the Headmaster - Dr Maurice Denby. As the whole school stood to attention for assembly, Dr Denby used to leave his room, striding swiftly into the main hall carrying a book or a file under his arm and, with his head slightly on one side, wasted no time in taking his place on the rostrum at the end of the hall. With all the teachers gathered on either side of him across the hall and with all the boys facing him in absolute silence (or nearly so), who could be unimpressed by such a tense atmosphere? Quite a few of the boys, I'm afraid.

I only remember a single occasion when I was required to face Dr Denby because of a misdemeanour. I was pulled out of the line by a prefect as we were about to disperse, following morning assembly along with a few other miscreants. As everyone else filed out, I remember standing there in a line awaiting Dr Denby's punishment. I had offended by thoughtlessly going to school with dirty or unpolished shoes, and I received one stroke of Dr Denby's cane. This taught me one lesson anyway - 'NEVER LET THE PREFECTS CATCH YOU WITH DIRTY SHOES'.

NINETEEN

SUNDAY SCHOOL ANNIVERSARIES

As I approach my eighty-fifth birthday, there is no doubt in my mind that the most important influence in my life, apart from that of my parents and my own family, has been the Christian Church, and the Methodist Church in particular.

At the beginning of this account of my early life, I wrote that I was born into a strong chapel-going family, and that we attended the Primitive Methodist Chapel in School Street, Low Moor. My father was Choirmaster and Organist, and both he and my grandfather taught in the Sunday School. It was quite normal in those days for me to attend chapel services twice each Sunday, as well as Sunday School, morning and afternoon. One might think that I would feel that this was a bit much, but on the contrary, until I was well into my 'teens, I accepted this way of life and indeed, enjoyed it.

When my sister was a baby and my mother was confined to the house, I was taken to chapel by my father, no doubt to keep me out of my mother's way, but I grew up to enjoy the singing and soon learned to share in the hymn-singing myself, in such old favourites as 'Yield not to Temptation' and 'Sound the Battle Cry'. For a time I sat in the choir stalls, on the tenor side, next to my dad who was seated on the organ stool.

Next to me sat James Bottomley and Jimmie Stead, while on the seat in front of us sat Willie Taylor. I remember that sometimes I was allowed to sit next to my Dad on the organ stool, and occasionally I was permitted to operate the Swell pedal for him, but I can't remember what the occasions were when I was allowed to do that; I can't think that it was in the course of a normal service. I think it more likely that these adventures occurred when I was down at church with my dad when he was making adjustments to the organ, possibly after the electric blower had been fitted.

It was a very old and weary two-manual organ and I know that my father spent many hours with wire and string, coaxing a few more years of life out of the failing instrument.

Often, the only encouragement needed to keep him working on the old organ, was for someone to volunteer to 'blow' the organ, and often I was the reluctant 'volunteer'. It was quite a hard task for a little fellow, in fact almost too much.

Occasionally I used to be required to pump the handle when my dad was inside the instrument repairing the bellows, but when he was trying out the organ from the keyboard, he tended to get carried away, forgetting who was blowing the organ. At such times, all I could do when I had no more strength left, was to allow the lead weight (which indicated how much 'wind' was in the bellows) to rise to the top of the marked board and stay there. When that point was reached, the sound of the organ used to die away, with a tremendous sigh.

After a while, of course, when I was getting stronger, these situations did not arise, and then to everyone's joy (especially my dad's) the chapel was able to afford to have an electric blower fitted. After which, he was able to go down to chapel to play the organ just when he wanted, and for as long as he chose.

In the early days when I was sitting in the choir stalls Mr Taylor, by way of keeping me occupied, used to write little notes which he passed over to me in the course of the service. Very naughty of him, really. I used to read these notes, sometimes with difficulty, but as my skill in reading and writing improved I used to reply to his queries in my childish hand. Usually this activity was sufficient to keep me quiet during the sermon.

Although, as I have said, we were a committed Primitive Methodist family, we enjoyed cordial relations with our friends and neighbours of the Wesleyan Reform Chapel in Albert Street - 't'Tin Chapel' - as it was generally known.

I considered it to be quite an occasion, when I was old enough to attend the Wesleyan Reform Sunday School Anniversary, which was held (and still is) on the third Sunday in June.

Owing to the chapel premises being so small the services were held (weather permitting) in the field adjoining the chapel and at the rear of the mill. The augmented choir occupied a platform which had been erected in tiers up to the rear wall of the mill. The singing was accompanied by an amateur orchestra, seated in front of the choir.

How strange it seems nowadays, when we see the old photographs of these gatherings, with the women wearing HUGE hats and most of the men in bowler hats, with just a few in straw hats or boaters and this event, we must remember, was held in the open air.

As far back as I can remember, my father always went along to assist in the choir, while the rest of us, together with our neighbours, went along to swell the congregation. Our own Sunday School Anniversary was always held in May, and it was well supported by our friends from the Wesleyan Reform Chapel. We used to close our own chapels for each other's Sunday School Anniversary evening services.

The 'Prims' Chapel, being considerably larger than the 'Tin Chapel', was able to accommodate any number who were likely to attend in addition to an augmented choir of perhaps sixty or seventy children and adults, though I do remember one or two occasions when chairs had to be placed down the aisles.

In the 1920's it seemed that the leaders of the Sunday School were not content to have the Anniversary Services only on the Sunday, but frequently there was a Sunday School Demonstration on the Saturday evening, such as 'The Building of the Cross'.

I can still recall one memorable line from such a performance. It was spoken by Joe Stobart, who wasn't very old at the time, perhaps five years of age. The line, which he delivered with force, if in a staccato manner, sounded like this - 'AS A MAN' (Pause)'THINKETH' (Pause) 'IN HIS HEART'(Pause) 'SO IS HE'.

Sometimes the preacher on the Sunday would be one of the popular preachers from London (where else?), who would also deliver a lecture on the Monday evening.

What times we youngsters had learning all the items which we had to sing or recite; all carefully rehearsed at home with the aid of our parents. Reading lines from bits of paper was never considered for a moment in those days. All children were expected to learn the words they were given - and generally, we did.

Great days, when it seemed that everyone connected with the Sunday School, however loosely, and not forgetting parents who rarely ventured inside the walls of the church, all were happy to be involved in some activity. The Sunday School Anniversary was certainly an occasion of much devoted service and joyful enthusiasm in those days. Times change - not always for the better, one feels.

TWENTY

CONCLUSION

The time has now come for me to draw to a close this collection of memoirs, but I do so in the knowledge that I have already written an account of the second stage of the journey. This second stage was, as a matter of fact, written first (which is perhaps, a little unusual.).

As I have already mentioned, the book 'Towards Little Germany' was my first - though still unpublished at the time of writing this material. The book covers the first phase of my experience as an office worker in Little Germany, directly after leaving school.

It may be that readers who are themselves students of Local History will find omissions, repetitions and inaccuracies galore in both books. If I had the time, (and who can be sure of that?) I would have spent a lot more of it on research in the Reference Library and elsewhere, but at my age, I decided to 'make do' as we say in Bradford, with what was readily available, mainly in my memory.

I hope, therefore, that I may be forgiven for any errors of fact and that such misdemeanours will not so mar the book as to diminish its contribution to the personal histories of Low Moor.

When I left my school days behind me, to face a most uncertain future, this was the time when all the influences that had surrounded my earlier life came together, though I was quite unaware of this fact at the time.

I came to realise that it was not for nothing that I had been brought up in a loving Christian home, which enabled me, in difficult circumstances, to look for the best and to seek to do the best.

I am grateful now for the moral standards which I was taught to strive for, if not always successfully, but those standards did prepare me for the rough and tumble of my very first job, as well as for the period of unemployment that followed in the thirties, with its many pitfalls for young people.

Many of those experiences are recorded in 'Towards Little Germany', which tells of my life as an office junior during the years 1927 - 1930.'

BIBLIOGRAPHY

'30 Villages from Hipperholme to Tong'
        by James Parker

'Low Moor - The Story of a Village'
        by Constance Myers

'The Church of England, the Methodists and Society 1700-1850'
        by Anthony Armstrong

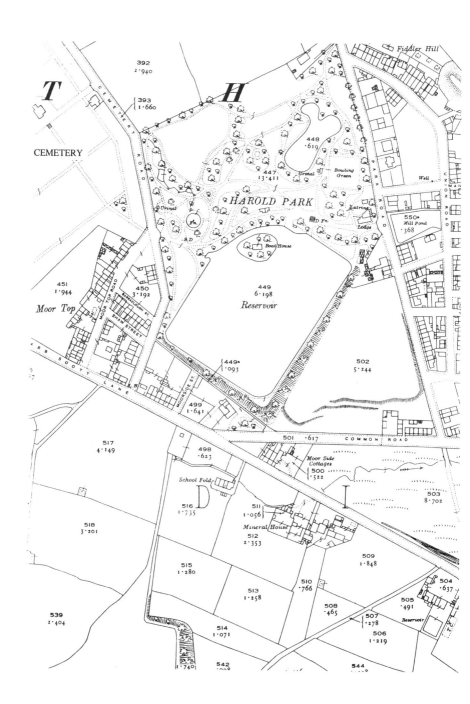

PHOTOGRAPHS

(1) - School Group
Taken in 1920 of Standard Four - Wyke Council School.
The author is at the far left of the second row.

(2) - Sunday School Group (1)
Taken in 1920 at the Sunday School Anniversary of School Street Primitive
Methodist Chapel, Low Moor. The author is second left in the third row.

(3) - Sunday School Group (2)
Taken in 1923 at the Adorning of the Cross at School Street Primitive
Methodist Chapel.
Back row : left to right
James Thorpe, Leslie Thorpe, Norman Ellis, William Stobart
Next to back row :
May Bottomley, Gertrude Smith, Evelyn Ellis (Bryon) (author's sister),
Eva White, Nellie Priestley (Stobart), Emily Platts (Fox), Edith Adams,
Agnes Fox (Barraclough),
Next to front row :
Renee Poole, ? Thorpe, Alice Airey, Lorna Benson , Joe Stobart, Agnes Stead,
Mary Dobson (Mounsey), Bertha Priestley,
Front row :
Elsie Dobson (Pearson), Dorothy Priestley, Eileen Bryden (Shaw),
Eileen (?) Benson, Lily Pearson, ? Thorpe, Victor Bartle, ? Smith.

(4) - Wright's Shop Group
Taken in black smith's shop commonly called the ' Wright's Shop' which was
within the buildings still standing at the junction of Huddersfield Road and Abb
Scott Lane. The author's grandfather, Garfitt Ellis, is second from the right.

(5) - School Street Primitive Methodist Church
Built in 1870 to replace an earlier building, later converted to cottages. The
frontage of this building collapsed in 1947 and the society moved to the Oxley
Place premises. This building was later used as industrial premises and
demolished along with much of Low Moor in the early 1970's. (The first
Primitive Chapel in Low Moor stood on the site of Hill Top School.)

(6) - Union Street
Looking towards Mill Street showing the New Inn and part of Victoria Mills - taken in the 1960's. Now demolished.

(7) - Oxley Place Sunday School, School Street (now demolished)
Built in 1844, re-built 1859. Originally a branch Sunday School of Wesley Place Wesleyan Chapel and later Oxley Place Methodist Church. In 1970 it became Aldersgate Methodist Church when the congregations of Oxley Place and Wesley Place combined prior to erecting a new building at the junction of Common Road/Cleckheaton Road in 1974.

(8) - Fountain Street (1)
The street where the author lived as a boy. Now demolished.

(9) - Fountain Street (2)
Basement dwelling at the rear of Fountain Street where the author's aunt lived. Now demolished.

(10) - North Street
Looking towards Manor Row. Now demolished.

(11) - Manor Row
The houses behind the low cottages at the left are still standing.

(12) - Union Road
Today all the property on the left has disappeared but the Wesleyan Reform Chapel and the houses on the right still stand.

(13) - Huddersfield Road
The sign of the British Queen public house (still standing) gives an indication of the site of this photograph. The nearest house on the right was the former Liberal Club and became the home of George Booth the undertaker. Note also the Lion Stores which stood at the corner of School Street and the Victoria Hotel.

(14) - Low Moor Picture House *(1996)*
The building still stands and is now used as business premises.

(15) - Fly Wheel *(1996)*
A reminder of Low Moor's glory days. Can be found at the junction of New Works Road and Huddersfield Road.

(16) - Nos 1 to 3 Abb Scott Lane *(1996)*
Formerly known as Carter Fold. These buildings housed shops of the Low Moor Company. The cottages are associated with John Wesley's visit to Low Moor.

(17) - Mineral House *(1996)*
Originally built for the Low Moor Company's Mining Engineer.

(18) - School Fold *(1996)*
Originally a barn, this building was converted, by permission of the Low Moor Company, for use by the early Methodists, and was later used as a school.

(19) - Shaw Street *(1996)*
Where the author lived as a boy.

(20) - Moor Top Road *(1996)*
Cottages near the author's boyhood home.

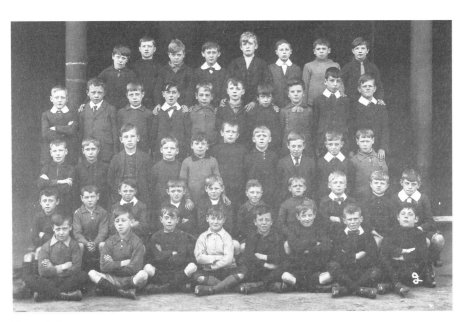

School Group

Sunday School Group 1

Sunday School Group 2

Wright' s Shop Group

School Street Primitive Methodist Church

Union Street

Oxley Place Sunday School, School Street

Fountain Street

Fountain Street (2)

North Street

Manor Row

Union Road

Huddersfield Road

Low Moor Picture House (1996)

Fly Wheel (1996)

Nos 1 to 3 Abb Scott Lane (1996)

Mineral House (1996)

School Fold (1996)

Shaw Street (1996)

Moor Top Road (1996)